VICTIM
SURVIVOR
CELEBRANT

THE HEALING
JOURNEY FROM
CHILDHOOD
SEXUAL ABUSE

VICTIM
SURVIVOR
CELEBRANT

THE HEALING
JOURNEY FROM
CHILDHOOD
SEXUAL ABUSE

ROBERTA NOBLEMAN

Abbey Press

© 1994 by Roberta Nobleman
Published by One Caring Place
Abbey Press
St. Meinrad, Indiana 47577

Library of Congress Catalog Number
94-072394

ISBN 0-87029-249-8

Cover by Scott Wannemuehler
Figures from *Tam Lin* by Jean Stufflebeem

Printed in the United States of America

THANK YOU,
FELICE

TABLE OF CONTENTS

ACKNOWLEDGMENTS

Prologue: Phyllis Cardona, Marie, Mary Virginia, Pam, Vicky.

Chapter I: David Finkel, Richard Strelecki, Guy, Carol Poston, Virginia Woolf, Jean Shinoda Bolen, St. Teresa of Avila, Julian of Norwich.

Chapter II: My brother Bill, his wife Isabelle, and their eleven children, Julia Lee DeLisle, my brother Bruce, his wife Margaret, and their three children.

Chapter III: Harriet Jacobs, Peri Aston (Joan), Mary Elizabeth Coleridge, *Book of Common Prayer*, *Daughters of Sarah* magazine, Susannah Wesley.

Chapter IV: Louis MacNeice, Sister Agnes Mallner, O.S.U., Sister Gerri McCullagh, Ann, Pat Ferry, the Psalmists, Clifton Anderson.

Chapter V: Alice Miller, Jessica, Ann from Ireland, J. Janda, Julie Keefer.

Chapter VI: Anton Chekhov, Bronx Zoo, Sister Ave Clark, O.P., *Wing Span*, Anne Sexton, Liza, Ann Ownbey, *The Other Side*, Brother Lee Brunner, Beethoven, Toni Morrison, John Shea, Betsy Beckman, Sister Peg Widman, R.S.M., Sister Connie Supan, I.H.M., Frances Giffin.

Chapter VII: Shakespeare, Jake.

Chapter VIII: Charles Dickens, Brother Joseph, O.C.S.O., monks of St. John the Evangelist, Abbot Francis Kline, O.C.S.O., Abraham Heschel, my "guys" at A.D.T.C., John Donne.

Chapter IX: Esther de Waal, Gustav Mahler, English Quaker writer, Abbot Andrew Giles, Cliff Ettinger, Sister Irene Mahoney, O.S.U., Father Edward, O.C.S.O.

And: Maury, Missy, Celia, Paul.

FOREWORD

R oberta Nobleman is a woman of rare courage. Her book is
about child abuse. If one is to enter into her world of
expression, one should also see her play, *Masks and
Mirrors*.

Watching her drama, I was struck by her message of forgiveness, even as she dramatizes the ugliness of the abuse which she
endured as a child. One of the subplots of her play, in fact, is the
journey of forgiveness—a kind of inverse development of the
story's obvious course.

The first great moment of the inverse maturity is the forgiveness of the abuser. But, then, one must confront one's own sense
of guilt and shame, where the next step is forgiveness of oneself.
For many of us, that second step looms larger than the first and

obvious move of leaving off being an adversary.

The third step is the mystical one. Here, one does not merely abandon the pain of the initial abuse, but one lives with it by transforming it in one's own being. Like the risen Christ, who, as the Lamb of God, appears in the heavenly liturgy with the marks of slaughter upon him, we too can wear our wounds as a sign of that ultimate mercy which Christ came to give to our world. For now, as Roberta reminds us, we are big enough and availed of sufficient strength to sustain the hate and violence and transform it into love.

The richness of Roberta's doctrine enkindled my energy and riveted my attention all during the play. Roberta has a message worthy of patristic theology. And she has transferred that integrated, miraculous, simultaneously inner-and-outward awareness to her book.

In *Masks and Mirrors*, Roberta enlists ancillary agents to co-address the audience. A Mozart clavier duet, written when the composer was age ten, represents the innocent child. Mahler's Second Symphony (*Resurrection*), which accompanies the depiction of abuse and the journey to forgiveness, fills the room with anguish and hope at the same time. At the end, the Mahler alternates with a Mozart symphony, the great G Minor, and the contrast indicates the levels of forgiveness.

From Mahler's pain, and the tortured sunshine at the cloud's edge, we move to the clear serenity of full light in Mozart and the recovery, now transformed, of the innocence of the child. Pain has been not removed but changed. It has been not avoided but overcome. Mozart, by some miracle of God, has forged a solution to the problems inherent in his material. Hope has seen him through. His vision of the transcendent end does not forsake him. But Mozart is all the richer after the weeping and humanity of Mahler. We need all of music for any of it to articulate its message.

Whether it be music or stories and images of animals, as in this book, Roberta weaves her materials into one powerful focus. Hers is a skillful assemblage of feeling and looking, touching and tasting and hearing. Her truth is universal human truth as it seeks the Divine Truth.

You will meet Roberta in this book, and you need, not cognitive preparation, but a sympathetic space where all your resources stand at attention to reaffirm you, as you traverse the painful, obscure journey to the light. She will make the trip deliciously pleasant—even irresistible—but dreadfully focused on that place of self-knowledge, horror, and anguish. She will lead you through to a sober, mature, yet childlike embrace of the Truth.

—*Right Reverend Francis Kline, O.C.S.O.*
Abbot, Mepkin Abbey
Moncks Corner, South Carolina

PROLOGUE

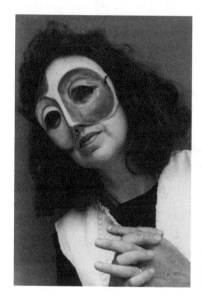

The author wearing her True Self mask, as photographed by her husband, Maurice Nobleman.

When I was growing up in England during the Second World War, everything was rationed. There were very few choices and very few brand names. Margarine was "special." I don't remember any other kind. Above the sink in the kitchen was a large tin of the one and only healing cream I knew as a child: a white, zinc-based ointment called by the exotic name "Zambuk"—good for hurt knees, bee stings, cuts, and diaper rash. I understand that the first-aid person who stands by at public events in Australia is called the "zambuk"—the one who has the healing salve available and is ready and appointed to apply it when needed.

On these pages, I want to explore the healing role of the "zambuk" as it applies to those of us who are adult survivors of childhood sexual abuse.

I am an actress. I know "actor" is the late twentieth century correct term for a female performer, but I don't feel like Robert DeNiro; I feel like Sarah Bernhardt. I specialize in one-woman shows. I woke up one day to the realization that my acting/teaching is my vocation—a serious, joyous, hilarious, inconvenient, exhausting, difficult gift for which I am most grateful.

For several years I had told other women's stories. Some famous, like St. Teresa of Avila. Some infamous, like Rev. Jeannette Piccard. But many unknown, unnamed, and unsung, like St. Peter's wife or St. Augustine's mistress. Now I knew that I had a story to tell too.

In my show *Masks and Mirrors*, I have sought to bring a little enlightenment to this dark and murky subject through telling my own story of sexual abuse as a child by my dad and the story of the famous English novelist Virginia Woolf, who was sexually abused by both her half-brothers during childhood and adolescence. In the final act of the show, I enact the roles of

• the enabler—the partner to the abuse, who through denial and avoidance "allows" the abuse to happen (in my case, my mother), and

• the perpetrator—the abuser, who for many complex reasons perpetuates the chain of abuse that somehow he or she received as a child (in my case, my father).

However, after I performed the show several times, a third most important character in this tragic scenario seemed to beg for recognition. I call him or her the zambuk. Let me quote from a letter, one of many that I have received:

> I was so glad to see *Masks and Mirrors*. You evoke much emotion with your movement and your words. It was hard for me to watch when you portrayed Virginia being sexually abused sitting up on the shelf. Last year, I found out that my seven-year-old daughter had been sexually abused by her grandfather. Shortly after that, I

found out that her fifteen-year-old sister had also been abused by him.

When my husband confronted his dad in March, he completely denied it. We continued to reassure our seven-year-old that we believed her. When we learned about our older daughter, we both confronted Pop in August. Even then, he continued for a time in his denial.

We have been trying ever since to get our lives back on an even keel. Fortunately, we are very much helped by an insightful, respectful therapist. I am currently working with him individually because of the painful memories of physical and emotional abuse from my own childhood.

I am at times overwhelmed and discouraged because there are so many needs to be met. I am learning to find supports and ask for what I need, but it is still so hard to do.

Perhaps now my question at the end of the performance makes some sense: "What did your mother do that helped?" I sometimes feel so totally inadequate. Only prayer sustains me and gives me the courage to continue to hope. Perhaps I too will find I am finally in the place where I should be.

In one-person theater, the audience co-creates with the performer. Audience members are drawn into the action, becoming the other characters in the drama, in a unique way. Whenever there are two or more actors on stage, the audience can sit back and say, "Entertain me!" Much more is demanded when everything that happens is between me and thee. The audience that *chooses* to come and see a show about childhood sexual abuse always has good reason to be there. I presume you are reading this book "because…"

After thousands of years of deathly silence in this grim area of childhood sexual abuse, finally our society is starting to speak out on the "last terrible taboo." With the widespread education of women (at least in the developed world), many of us are writing our own memories of abuse. Adult survivors of both sexes are beginning to name, to acknowledge, to proclaim what happened to them as children. In the last ten years, there has been a flood of literature about how to heal the wounds of sexual abuse. A small stream has even filtered into the realm of religious books and magazines. Most of these books are addressed to the victims themselves. This book is for them too, but the principal readers will be the zambuks of the world. Perhaps a second subtitle for this book—in addition to *The Healing Journey from Childhood Sexual Abuse*— could be:

> **What victims/survivors of childhood sexual abuse would like their friend, spouse, fiancé(e), counselor, therapist, bishop, favorite aunt, second cousin, spiritual director, minister, priest, neighbor, chiropractor, secretary, best buddy, lawyer, superior, congressman or congresswoman, hairdresser, gynecologist-obstetrician, dentist, sister-in-law, chief of police, most reliable babysitter, the man who exercises next to them at the spa, the woman who works with them at the soup kitchen, and especially the person in the next pew at church...to know and understand, but somehow could not bring themselves to say.**

There may be thousands of you lying in bed at night worrying, praying: "Where is the salve I can provide? What can I do? How can I help?"

One day after my show, a woman came up to me in great distress. Pointing to the mask of the enabler, she blurted out, "I'm her!" As I listened to the story of her brother's abuse of her two nieces, I realized that she was not the enabler, because she was entirely innocent of the abuse. The brother and his wife lived several hundred miles away. The wife felt totally powerless; she called her poor sister-in-law daily, expecting her to do something. Should she call the police on her brother? Should she confront him herself? Should she tell her parish priest, call a family therapist? She herself was scheduled for surgery the next week, and the thought of entering the hospital with this dreadful burden was leaving her wretched and sleepless. She desperately needed an "inn" where other capable hands could take the burden of the wounded ones from her.

A young man engaged to be married suddenly finds out that his bride-to-be is no virgin, for she lost her virginity to his future father-in-law at the age of eight. The wedding is only two months off; his bride tells him she cannot bear to be touched intimately. The fiancé confides in the priest who is to marry them, who throws up his hands in horror. Everyone is giving him advice, including his fiancée's therapist. What is to happen now?

An actively homosexual man enters a monastery and finds the abbot to be somewhat in denial as to the ways of the world (a perfect enabler). He seduces an older monk who entered very young and innocent and is now feeling lonely and at a low ebb in his spiritual life. The abuse continues for eighteen months, when at last the victim sees his way clear to say "no." The abuser, by this time, has also approached other monks and finally leaves the monastery. A few years later, another abbot comes to office, inheriting the aftermath of this devastation. How is he to respond when he becomes aware of the abuse? Does he merely say, "That was some years ago. It won't happen again while I'm here, and the victims seem to have recovered…"? But have they? And how can he be sure it will never happen again? What is he to do?

I think of a two-hour phone call I had with a woman who worked as a secretary at a seminary, the mother of ten children, all grown, a very good Catholic woman whose husband was, not cruel, but cold and distant, outwardly pious—he attended Mass daily—a pillar of the church. Just before Christmas, one of the daughters informed the woman that she had been abused by her father when a child. The mother courageously gathered all the family together and confronted the father, who, of course, denied it in spite of the fact that another daughter admitted that she too had been abused. The family divided into two camps, those who sided with the father, those who sided with the mother. Over Christmas, the mother almost committed suicide. In the end, she persuaded her husband to contact a priest at the seminary known for his experience in dealing with problems of human sexuality. Unfortunately the priest was not wise in this situation and did not know who to believe. The father took this as absolution of guilt and the mother is left to this day in abject despair and with a family in devastation. Where could she turn for help?

"Who is my neighbor?" asked the lawyer of Jesus. He replied with a parable—The Good Samaritan. What can I expect from this wounded traveler? asked the Good Samaritan. How can the Samaritan preserve his own "goodness"? Where are his healing oils, her wine and bandages, and the means of transportation? Let me respond with a parable.

Tam Lin

The Scottish border ballad of *Tam Lin* was collated by Sir Walter Scott from the printed and oral versions collected by him. He published it in his *Minstrelsy of the Scottish Border* in 1802-1803. The version presented here was retold in modern English by Kevin Crossle-Holland.

The ballad begins with a warning given to all maidens not to cross the plain of Carterhaugh, for fear of young Tam Lin, lest they leave "their rings or green gowns/Or else their maidenhood." Fair Janet, however, takes up the challenge and ventures into the plain. Her first sally alerts Tam Lin to the trespass, and when, in her second foray, she plucks roses from the tree by the well, Tam Lin appears, "a little wee man/At lady Janet's knee." True to the warning, he takes her without her leave, and she returns to her father's hall carrying his child. Time passes, and:

Janet put on her green green dress,

Nine months were nearly gone,
And she set off for Carterhaugh
To talk with young Tam Lin.

She had scarcely picked two roses,
Two roses and their thorns,
When up sprang the little wee man:
"Lady, you'll pick no more.

Why are you picking roses, Janet,
In this bright green glade?
Do you mean to kill the pretty child
We two together made?"

"O you must tell me how, Tam Lin,
And not one word a lie;
Have you ever set foot in a chapel?
And have you been baptized?"

"I'll tell you the truth, Janet,
And not one word a lie.
You're the child of a lady and knight,
And the same is true of me.

My grandfather was Roxburgh,
I lived with him as a child,
This accident befell me then
As we rode home from the field:

Roxburgh was a hunting man
And loved riding to his hounds
And on a cold and frosty day
I was thrown to the ground.

The Queen of Fairies caught me up
And took me into that hill,

I'm a fairy head and toe,
Fair lady, look at me well.

The fairy land is beautiful
But, terrible to tell,
Every seven years,
We pay a tithe to hell;
And I'm so strong-bodied and fair
I fear it'll be myself.

Tonight is Hallowe'en, lady,
Tomorrow is All Hallows.
Win me, win me, if you will.
You have no time to lose.

In the dark, at the hour of midnight,
The fairy folk take horse,
And she who would win her true-love
Must wait at Miles Cross."

"But how will I know you, Tam Lin?
How can I be quite sure
Among so many strange knights
I've never seen before?"

"When the first troop comes riding by,
Say nothing, let them pass;
When the next troop comes riding by,
Say nothing, let them pass;
Then a third troop will come riding by—
I'll be one of those.

Oh! Let the black horse pass, lady,
And then ignore the brown,
But quickly grasp the milk-white horse
And pull the rider down.

For I'll be riding the milk-white horse,
The rider nearest the town.
Because I was christened as a knight,
They granted me that boon.

My right hand will be gloved, lady,
My left hand will be bare;
The peak of my cap will be turned up,
And I'll comb down my hair.
These are the signs I'll give to you;
Without fail I'll be there.

Lady, they'll turn me in your arms,
Into an **eft** and **adder**;
But hold me fast, don't let me pass,
I am your baby's father.

They'll turn me into a **cruel bear**
And then a **mighty lion**;
But hold me fast, don't let me pass,
As you love your own scion.

And then they'll turn me in your arms
Into **red-hot iron**:
But hold me fast, don't let me pass,
I'll cause no hurt or harm.

First dip me in a bowl of milk
And then a bowl of water;
But hold me fast, don't let me pass,
I'll be your baby's father.

And next time they turn me in your arms
Into a **toad** and then an **eel**;
But hold me fast, don't let me pass,

If you but love me well.

They'll turn me in your arms, Janet,
Into a **dove** and then a **swan**;
And last they'll turn me in your arms
To a mother-naked man.
Cover me with your green cloak—
I'll be my own True Self again."

Gloomy, gloomy was the night
And eerie the sheen on the grass,
As Janet donned her green cloak
And walked to Miles Cross.

At the dead hour of the night
She heard the bridles ring;
She was as glad to hear them
As any earthly thing.

First she let the black horse pass,
Then ignored the brown,
But quickly she grasped the milk-white horse
And pulled his rider down.

She pulled him from the milk-white horse
And let the bridle fall;
And there rose up a ghastly cry:
"He's stolen from us all!"

They turned him in fair Janet's arms
Into an eft and adder;
She held him fast in every shape
To be her baby's father.

They turned him in her arms at last
To a mother-naked man

She wrapped him in her green cloak,
As blithe as a bird in spring.

Then the Queen of Fairies she spoke out,
From within a bush of rye:
"She's taken away the fairest knight
In my whole company.

Had I known, Tam Lin,
A lady would borrow thee,
I would have taken away your two grey eyes,
Put in two eyes of tree!"

"Had I known, Tam Lin," says she,
"Before ye came from home,
I would've taken out your heart of flesh,
Put in a heart of stone!"

This poem is from my own British Isles. A story from our own roots is often the best. Much as I can identify with Celie's feelings in *The Color Purple*, the milieu in which the story takes place, a southern black community, is not familiar to me. But castles—I grew up with them. I am like Teresa of Avila, who wrote of an "Interior Castle." The castle of Carterhaugh, as depicted in *Tam Lin*, is home ground for me. The county of Kent, in the south of England, where I grew up, has more castles per square mile than any other place on earth. We used to play in the ruined castle of Tonbridge as children. Janet's journey is mine too. The Queen of Fairies (the dark side of ourselves that we must encounter, especially in "the dark, at the hour of midnight") is the wicked witch who still shrieks in my ears and challenges me though all the turning phases of my life.

Yet I am the heiress of Carterhaugh, and I am pregnant with new life now. The two roses (and their thorns) are mine for the picking. My green, green cloak is my priestly robe, lined with dark shadows that contain within the folds all the rare and rich efts and adders, swans and cruel bears, red-hot irons, lions, doves, and toads. Who is Tam Lin—the mother-naked man? For me, it is Christ—the naked man who hung as victim on the cross, but broke through to Resurrection. Others may name their lover, their "Messiah" differently: Allah, the Compassionate One; "God within myself and love her fiercely," says Shug in *The Color Purple*; my True Self, the individuated balance of anima and animus; "my still waters," wrote the Psalmist; "the place just right," said the author of "Simple Gifts." But the urgent appeal is always the same: "Hold me fast, don't let me pass." This is true not only for Janet, but for all who are touched by her story—and who want to be supportive and caring. We need you.

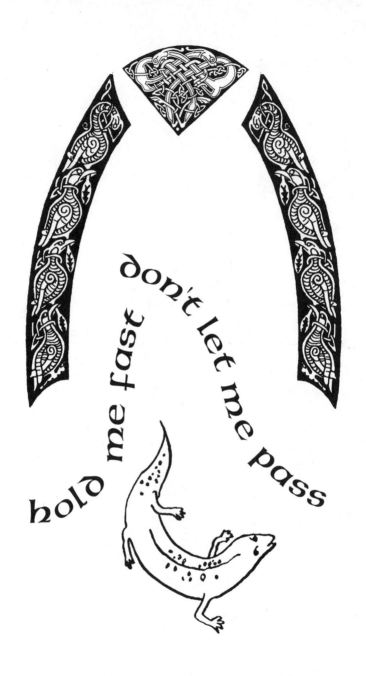

hold me fast don't let me pass

I THE EFT:

REMEMBERING THE PAIN, BREAKING THROUGH THE DENIAL

When I started performing J. Janda's play *Julian* in 1983, I realized that her story was in some ways *my* story. *Why* did this great woman mystic of the thirteenth century desire, pray for, the Revelations of Divine Suffering? Was it mere coincidence that she had survived three outbreaks of the plague—at age six, age twenty, and close to the time of her visions at age thirty-and-a-half? In rehearsals, I had already written my biography of Julian's life, which included childhood suffering, widowhood, the death of her child, and constant difficulties with her mother and father. I knew that if I was to play Julian with any integrity, I needed spiritual direction myself.

My second spiritual director, Brother Timothy, O.H.C., an

Anglican monk, would meet me once a month at General Seminary on Ninth Avenue and 20th Street in New York City. About a year into my meetings with Timothy, he asked me for a lift in my car to the Cathedral of St. John the Divine, on 110th Street. Just as he was getting into the car, he said, "I am hearing so much about child sexual abuse in spiritual direction these days and the church must do something about it."

I suddenly blurted out, "That happened to me, Timothy!" He took the news much more seriously than I had intended. "What have you done about it?" he asked over the roof of the car. To defuse the bomb that had exploded between us, I quickly got into the car and announced lightly, "That was all a long time ago! I don't know what made me ever mention it. It's all over and forgotten now. I don't wish to speak of it anymore."

But Timothy did! He nagged me for eighteen months, bringing up the issue every time I went for spiritual direction, until at last I said, "Look, I *don't* want to talk about this. It doesn't matter. It's *over!*" Sitting there in his white monk's robe, he replied, "Your father violated you and it doesn't matter?" I began to cry. It had just begun.

Efts are adolescent newts, little reptiles that live in shallow waters and may suddenly appear on land. We all have to come to that place where we are ready "to go down to Carterhaugh" and take the risk. What triggers sexual abuse memories after they have been repressed for so many years? These little snippets of memories, like the efts, lie in the shallow waters of the unconscious and usually emerge at a time when we are ready to deal with them. Flashbacks are the term used by survivors. A vivid picture, like a camera flash, suddenly pops into the mind, unbidden, often triggered by something as elusive as a smell or the color of a curtain fluttering in the breeze, or the way a man reaches for a piece of fruit, and then the memory drops away unexpectedly.

After my own abuse stopped, in my early teens, I let it all slip into my pre-conscious. I knew it had happened, but I was not ready for it to be verbalized. This splitting-off process, when, in effect, we put the wound on a shelf in the back of the mind or down in the basement of the unconscious, is the psyche's way of dealing with the trauma. Yes, I did act it out by being a fairly difficult teenager. My mother went into a deep depression, and my father made the best of it by running away whenever he could to go fishing or to the dog races or wherever he could escape the boredom and misery of work and home. What he really wanted to do was go back to India where he had been a soldier for over twenty years in a life of great adventure. There he killed tigers in the jungle, fished the rivers, guarded Gandhi during the time of his house arrest, and had a reputation as comedian par-excellence. During those black-and-white sixteen millimeter films shown to the troops in the jungle, Dad stood by the screen making all the voices and orchestrating the audience in sound effects, songs, and general merriment.

Two weeks after the dreadful earthquake in Quetta, in the north of India, Dad had already improvised a show to lift the spirits of soldiers and earthquake victims alike. It was called "Cinderella Reconstructed," and, for me, represents his entire outlook on life: Yes, bad things happen, but in the midst of the ruin and devastation is the clown begging us to be brave and smile that we have survived. "I piped for you, but you would not dance," says Jesus. My dad was a piper without a flute or an audience in those days when I was an adolescent in the home above the news agent's shop at 152 London Road.

So, I had two different role models to deal with life's pain. Caught between them, I favored my father's way and, fortunately, I had the support system of an excellent education in an all girls' school with one or two teachers who encouraged creativity; friends, Ann, Jean, Sally, Jen; cousins, aunts and uncles, a granddad who I adored. But above all, I had my imagination and my acting. There was a healthy place to run away to.

After three years of theater school training (ages seventeen to twenty) it all flowered into exciting and challenging jobs that involved much travel: Scotland, Paris (the Sorbonne

University—I won a scholarship there), Israel, Canada (I was a director at the Manitoba Theatre Centre in Winnipeg for four years), and finally to America and marriage. When I was twenty-eight, I gave birth to my first child, Melissa. In the years when my three children were small and I was living the life of a suburban housewife, mother, and teacher, there were certainly the tag-ends of the childhood abuse.

From time to time, they intruded in my life: why was I so petrified at the thought of driving a car or learning to type? (I flunked typing classes at the local adult evening school three times!) Why did I choose to direct the play *Ghosts* by Henrik Ibsen and Brecht's *Galileo* when I was teaching at Fairleigh Dickinson University? Both plays are about power issues, and the former is a story of incest. Looking back, I see many, many clues that led to that moment on my fortieth birthday when I suddenly burst into tears and wept inconsolably for a long time. A few months later, I had another huge weep at Ithaca College after listening to a Jewish storyteller with a tale of terrible abuse that somehow felt like my story too. Above all, there was the sense that from time to time, I seemed to get in my own way, and I did not know why. The head of my department at Fairleigh Dickinson University said that he did not appreciate my "unbuttoned ways." For the past twelve years, I have been examining these "buttons" and the corresponding "holes" and, where necessary, buttoning them up!

In order to find a handle to turn the door and take a first peek at the vast devastation of child abuse, we need a rough, and necessarily inaccurate, framework in which to place the door itself. The splitting-off that is a result of the abuse is an adaptive mechanism, but it wreaks havoc in the life of the adult. By the time the first flashbacks (efts) have surfaced, the pond may be very murky indeed. The younger the victim, the muddier the pond. If the damage was done to a toddler, there may be many different "selves" that developed as the child grew and, in cases of severe wounding, even a borderline personality where everything is dichotomized. Already, at the eft stage, we may be touching the tip of the rage iceberg. A kind of fundamentalist approach ensues. Everything is seen in black or white, no in between.

I would like to visualize three contexts in which the adult victim might find him or herself. Three houses, if you will, situated around the lake of memories. Some of us are situated clearly in the center of one particular house; others may be lurking in the doorway or the back bedroom; still others are on the far side of the pond, but with a direct view of one or other of the "houses." Some may inhabit more that one home.

In the first category, the adult victim seated at the center of the house might say, "My memories are so awful, so repulsive to me; therefore all sexual activity is bad. I want no part of any of it." This, at its extreme, would make the choice of a celibate life style most attractive. This house of memories is often protected by many walls, fortressed by ivy-covered look-out towers, gates, and shutters. So when such a homeowner does allow you a peek through the grill, it is deemed a privilege that only a trusted person with the right credentials is granted. Monasteries, convents, seminaries, and missions have all provided haven for these souls. A shocked Puritan

A gargoyle depicting shocked clergy.

attitude in Protestant churches has been an umbrella under which spinsters, bachelors, and the unhappily married could find shelter. Our Victorian forbears venerated this kind of asexuality and named it chastity. It is rather like the heavy lead apron that is put round one's shoulders in the dentist's chair to protect us from the X-rays.

A perfect example of this was a sister I met who came to a summer institute on sexuality because there were glimmers of uneasiness in her life (and her superior sent her!). She imagined herself as the long, pink, nicely ironed, buttoned-to-the-neck flannel night gown that hung in her room untouched by any hand but her own, and "that," she said, "is the way I always want it to be, and no one is going to disturb that!"

Category one may include many people who do not go to the far extreme of abhorring all sexuality, but there may still remain a tendency in this direction. These people often develop a split in the personality between an intellectual desire to have and to appreciate the erotic in life, but the other part of them that was so wounded as a child prevents them from actually achieving it. The message they give out to a would-be lover is, "If you love me, you won't have sex with me!" They may be cuddled and admired, but the moment this develops into sexual intimacy, they freeze up and push the person away. The body remembers what it wished it could say as the little girl or boy to the abuser, even as the intellect is saying, "I ought to enjoy this." It is a terrible dilemma for someone in a marriage to a survivor. What remedy for such a situation? A re-education of the body and much patience are needed. Find out what is acceptable to the survivor. For example, my abuse stopped before my breasts developed, so I don't have terrible flashbacks associated with that part of my body. Sometimes, the person who makes a big speech to me at the beginning of a retreat weekend ("I am not to be touched! Don't ever mention anything physical!") is the same person who at the end of the weekend, invites a hug and clings to me most desperately, crying out her need for some kind of intimacy. To bring together the two halves of this fragmented person means some very sensitive body work. Think of the Terence Rattigan film *Tea and Sympathy*, which dealt with this subject so delicately.

In the second house, the adult victim says, "My memories taught me that sex is the only thing that makes me feel powerful and alive and good about myself; therefore I need more and more of it to satisfy me and to take my revenge." At the center of such a house of ill repute sits the sex addict or prostitute repeating the sexual act several times a day with a variety of different partners.

If I had to choose one of these houses, I would say I have lived on the far side of the pond, occasionally feeling myself pulled relentlessly into house number two. Unlike house number one, this house is unprotected, doors and windows flung open in careless abandon. It is crowded with ten tons of furniture, bric-a-brac, and stuff—as messy as a teenager's bedroom, its drawers overstuffed and spilling out underwear, unmatched socks, and the intimate details of the owner's life on display for all to see. When the efts come crawling out of this part of the pond, they often come in battalions! The owner is often tempted to run away as fast as possible. Unfortunately, the efts follow after us.

As the nineteenth century society often encouraged people to dwell in house number one (celibacy as a "higher way of life"), so the late twentieth century entices us, through the media, into the hollow haven of house number two. Neither one is a healthy place to be.

In the second category, there often seems a compulsive repetition of sexual acting-out as survivors unconsciously try to master the trauma of their childhood. In seeking out all these different sexual partners, it almost seems as if they are attempting to de-traumatize sex. There have been countless stories of such people, and I suppose the best modern example is the movie *Nuts* with Barbra Streisand in the lead role. What could anyone who loved her and wanted to help her do in this case? We saw how the professionals (the therapists) in the film handled this prostitute who broke down in court and admitted her molestation as a child by her step-father. What could the character's best friend have done to intervene *before* she became so promiscuous? Perhaps understanding is the most important factor. So, let us imagine that Barbra's friend had also been abused as a child. How might the story have been different if she had intervened and shared her story so that Barbra did not have to go to jail and end up spilling it all out in front of a whole courtroom full of people?

In the third category, the victim says, "My memories taught me that I cannot trust or enjoy my sexuality except with a person of the same gender as myself, and I will compulsively seek satisfaction with as many partners as possible since society and the church denies me."

We are *not* debating the source of homosexual behavior between nature or nurture. By now, anyone reading the book will probably be familiar with the scientific evidence that suggests gay and lesbian people are born, not made that way. It is difficult in our homophobic society to distinguish any framework for this house, for it is shattered by vandals and covered in graffiti: "Death to fags, queers, dykes, etc." Even to write such words makes me feel dirty on the inside! Let me quote from research by David Finkel here:

> Boys victimized by older men were over four times more likely to be currently engaged in homosexual activities than were non-victims. Close to half the male respondents who had had a childhood sexual experience with an older man were currently involved in homosexual activity... [and] some data outside of our survey, as well as clinical evidence, suggest that one response to the trauma of incest is to turn away from heterosexuality and to embrace a lesbian orientation and life style. If such a relationship between incest and lesbianism exists, given the prevalence of homophobia in this society, this would indeed be evidence of the trauma of incest.

An in-depth study of adult gays and lesbians might uncover a good deal of childhood sexual abuse. The concern that this might add another burden to the family members who "ought," who "should" have protected the child is very real. But an assessment of this piece of very real estate is essential for the zambuk as he or she sits in the chair opposite the victim. Remember, too, that you may be one of the first to know, for a large and very nasty closet sits smack in the middle of house number three. You may be invited to step inside to hear the "confession," or you may have to listen on the threshold of the house because the victim is ready to slam the closet door in your face out of fear: What if you are like all the rest and cannot even countenance the childhood memories because of dealing with the discomfort of the disclosure of homosexuality?

The third category is difficult to write about, but it seems to me there are two sub-categories.

a) Those who are defending their sexuality against heterosexual condemnation (these are often extroverted people).

b) Those who say, this is purely my choice.

Either way, there is often a great deal of self-hatred that has to be worked through and also enormous sexual tension.

Take the example of E.M. Forster who wrote most eloquently of the erotic. If you think of that delicious movie *Room With A View* (a faithful version of the novel) and compare it with his suppressed novels about homosexual love, you will see what a wonderful, sensitive, wise, neutral observer this gay writer could be. My own warm and deep relationships with my gay brothers and sisters have been the most healing of all. How many times have I heard women exclaim, "How safe I feel with him; there's no tension there because he's gay!" But who can help the gay survivor of childhood abuse themselves? Probably someone like themselves but further along the journey to healing, or else a mature and wounded one who has gone deeply into his or her own pain.

If a gay person tells you about sexual acting-out that seems very alien to you and you are *covering up* being repulsed by it, you probably are not the right person to be there for them. Remember, too, that we all inherit a different set of values for gay people than for straight people. What might be "sowing his wild oats" for a straight man might be "lewd behavior" for a gay man.

All of these categories may ultimately lead to perpetuating the chain of abuse and to sexual acting-out with children— becoming the abuser or a very apt enabler, especially in category one.

It is not within the scope of this book to examine in depth the various ramifications of all this, but let us look at the response of the healer or "pro-survivor" to each of these "Three Classes of Men" (and Women), as St. Ignatius put it in his *Spiritual Exercises.*

Most important, I would ask you to consider your own sexuality before contemplating that of another. It is quite obvious that various pronouncements on sexual matters by leaders of all kinds, both in church and society, are often made by hurting "little boys" and "little girls" out of touch with all reality. Ask yourself (especially around 3 a.m.) "Who am I?" "How do I really feel, not think, about the place of sexuality in my life?" "When was I last in love?" "Is there a fear of the erotic—or a delight?" "Do I have any ambivalent feelings about my own sexual organs and things like menstruation or spontaneous erection?"

"The blind cannot lead the blind, lest they both fall into a ditch," said Jesus.

In St. Luke's Gospel we read that God created a situation for Jesus to be born into in which *two* women were pregnant in somewhat compromising situations. The angel messenger tells Mary that "her cousin Elizabeth, whom everyone considered barren is now in her sixth month, for with God, all things are possible." Why bother with this feminine detail of "the sixth month" if not to emphasize the physical aspects of Elizabeth's pregnancy?

Or, that Zechariah, supported by the prayers of all the men in the outer sanctuary, and with the vision of the angel still with him, should have returned home to make love to his elderly wife and conceive John the Baptist? Men (and I use the word exclusively!) have sometimes chosen to ignore the frail and tender sexuality that surrounds the stories of the Incarnation and substituted their own mythic projections. Women know that, having stayed with Elizabeth for three months, Mary had missed two periods, which in reality means that sometime around the seventh day after her last period was due, when there was still that morning no show of blood, when Mary's breasts were already feeling tingly and swollen, she went to Elizabeth who said, "My dear!

That's it!—exactly how it was with me! You had better return to Nazareth and tell Joseph."

Now, if in reading the last paragraph all kinds of signals were going on in your mind, such as "Mary didn't have a period! How could she mention anything as gross as Our Lady with Swollen Breasts!" or, if you happen to be from a Protestant tradition where Mary and Elizabeth are virtually ignored and your celibacy took the form of "maiden lady" (as spinsters were kindly called in the past) or "unmarried gentleman" (bachelor), then I believe you would do well to look at the avoidance, the "plank within your own eye, before attempting to remove the beam from another's."

We all play out our lives along a vast horizontal line of sexuality—at various places on the spectrum, including our heterosexuality or homosexuality. An asexuality that manifests itself as a kind of abhorrence of anything erotic is a sickness, and there is a cause. God may have created us with a low sexual drive, or we may have channeled all that sexual passion into something like music or science or art or, of course, a vocation. (Teresa of Avila and many mystics can attest to this.) Or it may be that, like St. Augustine, in the past we were compulsive, even addicted to sexuality. A drastic conversion experience, like that experienced by a St. Paul or a St. Augustine, can lead to the opposite extreme: "How sordid and filthy are the embraces of a woman!" wrote St. Augustine. "It is better to marry than to burn," wrote St. Paul. "St. Peter washed away the filth of his marriage with the blood of his martyrdom," wrote St. Peter Damian. But, if this asexuality manifests itself as a condemnation of other people, we have a serious problem—and so do the others who interact with us. Can someone who fears sexual intimacy for herself help to heal another such soul? I doubt it. Let us make up a possible scenario:

Diedre grew up on the farm in Ireland, the sixth child of a family of eleven. Mother always pregnant, and, for obvious reasons, frigid; Father always anxious and overworked and sexually frustrated. He takes out this frustration on the child, Diedre (and perhaps her sisters, too). At eighteen years of age, how wonderful for Diedre to escape to the convent, to hide her shameful secret, to be clothed from head to foot in that protective habit, and to be kept safe by the convenient grill. Only Father Malachy, the priest, reminds her of what she has now come to hate and despise—men. But this one is old and doddery, and Diedre, now Sister Baptista, can repress those terrible memories, and, gazing at the white alabaster statue of Our Lady, all in stone, flat-chested, and thoroughly "virginal," she can begin a new life.

What happens to her forty years later? Sister Diedre (she has returned to her baptismal name) is now out of the habit and in the freer atmosphere of the late twentieth century. She starts to remember her childhood. To whom should she go?

I think Sister Diedre should find herself another woman. She should *not* go to a man. Mary did not discuss her pregnancy with the local rabbi or even Zechariah, the priest. Likewise, a man in a similar situation should go to another man or do as St. Joseph did and rely on dreams and deliberation with the wise men of Nazareth. Who are these wise men or women?

a) Those who themselves may have experienced abuse but who have worked their way through the pain.

b) Those who know the situation (e.g. for Diedre, are familiar with Ireland and the Irish).

c) Those who can put the person in touch with the right kind of long-term therapy or counseling.

d) Those who will not attempt to wave a magic wand to make it all go away—people based in reality.

e) Those who have the foresight to say, "Blessed are you among women and blessed is the new life that is stirring within you."

f) Those who do *not* feel called to be "The Messiah" (more of this later).

Preferably this zambuk should be someone with the qualities of the virgin goddess Athena. In the book *Goddesses in Everywoman*, Jean Shinoda Bolen describes the ways in which the goddesses of ancient Greece and Rome are alive and working out their purposes in us today. There is a companion book, *Gods in Everyman*, by the same author, which is equally helpful for some men. I am Aphrodite, always falling in love, playing "the wench," plagued by sexual fantasies, the alchemic goddess. Through my art I have found a place for my passions. As a little girl I delighted in play and dress-up, running about in a pair of oversized high heels, and my mother's 1930s evening gowns and a ratty old feather boa. In the theater, with its red plush curtains and sensual cupids and dark warmth, I knew that the little girl who sat starry-eyed on the edge of her seat at the back of the highest balcony (in England, called "the gods"), had found her home. The silver asbestos safety curtain (which read "For Thine Especial Safety"), in case fire broke out and spread to the audience, assured me that this was "heaven." Heaven for me is "Theater," and one of the reasons I love my Anglican Church is because our liturgy is theatrical.

Perhaps you have already discerned that I would not be the right person for someone like Sister Diedre. I once had a long conversation with a Methodist missionary—a woman. As a sensitive and over-protected only child, her worst memory is of an older boy exposing himself to her in the playground at school, and from that moment on, she had an absolute horror of men's bodies. Certainly she had never allowed herself to fall in love, for the memory of "that awful, big, hairy, horrible . . . THING" made her shudder to this day. Now she knew that my abuser had been much more explicit (oral sex, penetration, and for several years). She also knew that I had been married for many years and that I obviously liked men. How could I survive? Ever enjoy "it"? She assumed, as many people do, that anyone who experiences sexual abuse as a child must grow up to hate sexual intercourse and be totally dysfunctional.

I was the wrong person for her. She needed someone like a librarian, not an actress. Acting is a *bodily* art form and, in many people's minds, too sensual. (Why else would people remove the Blessed Sacrament from the sanctuary when I perform my plays?) Think of Hollywood, Elizabeth Taylor and all those husbands, or the Samaritan woman at the well (no "maiden lady"!).

I played the wife role while other little girls played with dolls. By the time I was nine years old, I knew a great deal about how to please a man. What one learns as a child stays in the psyche and in the body. It is not surprising that many adult survivors become rape victims. Our body sends out signals. I have never been raped, but I've always fantasized I might enjoy it. Who can help me to channel my sexuality, my passion, in ways that are creative and harmless and keep me true to my marriage and my "self"? To integrate all of this into my life so that my sexuality does not take up a disproportionate and unhealthy place, I need passionate people like myself, but those who have tamed the dragon that would devour us. This is dangerous territory because we understand one another very well, and in a man/woman relationship we may easily fall in love with one another and then the fires are enflamed, and we both embark on our way through a forest fire of dynamic proportions! All kinds of boundaries must be set up, and, for trust to be restored, read "the swan" chapter of this book. Perhaps safest of all is to find a soul friend in category three.

Gay and lesbian people who have come to an acceptance of their sexuality and are out of the closet and in a healthy place with a support group of others (rare souls in our repressive and hypocritical society) are often the perfect help-mate for those in the other two categories. I have come to believe that homosexuality is a gift from God which has been horribly squandered, abused, misunderstood, and feared, particularly since Victorian times. We no longer burn "faggots" at the stake literally, but still the whole issue is blanketed with a vast net of deceit, lies, shame, and hypocrisy. My experience growing up in a theater school where more than half the student population was gay revealed to me that those in the first year who were into gay-bashing in its most virulent form were usually those who had a very tentative hold on their own sexual identity. "Methinks thou dost protest too much," I said, and now I wonder about the childhood of some of those who postured as the Big Macho Guys. It seemed like typical junior high behavior—much repression, much "acting out," a lot of denial. When such people are in leadership positions, it is no wonder that the category three adult survivor is wary! With Jesus they might cry out, "Woe unto you, hypocrites!" So, who can help them? Certainly a wise gay man or woman can be present to another's pain. But what of the rest of society? And the church? Who can crawl out from under the terrible net of ambivalence and stretch out the helping hand? Who can they trust? A gay man or woman overhears things such as: "But I can't think what homosexuals *do*! I can't even conceive that a man could be turned on by another man's body. And, as for lesbians, I shudder at the thought!"

I do not shudder, and I know from experience that, in this business, gay or straight, male or female, any race, creed, or orientation, we are united by *our pain.* Sexual abuse is an equal opportunity problem crossing all boundaries. Perhaps the depth of the pain is most important of all for helping a category three person. A "Samaritan" who knows what it is to be spat upon, despised, and rejected is going to identify with the wounded traveler more than the priest or the Levite. Who knows, maybe he was mugged himself?

Who can be a zambuk for category three survivors? I think a lighthearted person with a good sense of humor, appreciative of the relatedness of all things, one with no Big Agenda for herself or himself (or anyone else), a person you would *choose* as a good sister or brother. It is worthy of contemplation that so many brilliantly gifted people have also been gay. The arts, in particular, have a disproportionately large number of gay people. Like the Jews, could this possibly have something to do with the depth of suffering they have endured? Maybe humility is the most important aspect when listening to the painful memories of a gay person. To say, "I know what you went through" is a lie. You don't. There is no hierarchy in suffering, and we must be careful to *listen carefully.* In listening to the "efts" of all survivors, you may find your eyes filling up with tears, perhaps in memory of some forgotten pain in your own history, as well as in sympathy for the other. Remember that as the survivors' abuse was bodily, they may have a problem with being touched. Be respectful of this. Your desire to hug them or even hold their hand may be just that—*your* desire, not theirs. Ask them gently, "Would you like to be held?" Remember, the body does not lie, and you may know more of the other person's pain through watching and touching (or not touching) than through words. "Holding fast," as in the poem, should not be taken any more literally than anything else.

Let me give you a few examples of my own of "efts" that appeared suddenly on the surface of my psyche over the last few years, and think about how you would respond if I were telling you about them right now.

I was in a thrift store looking for some costumes for one of my shows and came across a large barrel of assorted pieces of fabric of all colors. Suddenly I picked up a piece of red fabric that made me reel against the shelf, grab for the nearest blouse, and pretend to try it on in the little curtained cubicle at the end of the store. How could I tell the woman in the thrift store that the fabric was exactly the shade and texture of the red curtain that I stared at as a child while my father performed oral sex on me at the top of the stairs before putting me to bed? Fortunately, I was well into my healing by then so I actually bought the red fabric and now use it as part of the curtain in my show about abuse, *Masks and Mirrors.*

Suppose you, my friend, my pro-survivor, had been with me in the thrift shop. How would you have responded? (Remember, I am category two, so I probably would have told you about it.)

Here's an eft story from category one. A nun is watching one of my shows (nothing to do with abuse), and at the end I am chatting with a group of sisters as this is part of an assembly for their congregation. I mention the word "virgin" and how it has difficult connotations for me as a survivor. Suddenly I see her blanch; she pushes away the offers of "What's the matter?" and stumbles to her room. Months later I receive a letter from her: "My amnesia of forty years dropped away. I am a victim of sexual abuse," she writes. Suppose you had been one of her sisters at that assembly and, concerned for her, you later went to her room and knocked on her door. What would you say or do for her?

Finally, a gay priest abused by his mother (and others) is brought to a hospital to administer the last rites to a woman who attempted suicide. The bits and pieces of her story that emerge are playing on his unconscious memories of sexual abuse. The next week he finds himself uncontrollably seized with bouts of weeping. He does not yet know in his conscious mind what his body already knows so well. To whom should he go to share these terrible feelings? Could he go to you?

My friend Carol Poston writes of the dilemma of the survivor in the dentist's chair, because the position of vulnerability and the usually male dentist looming over the patient bring back familiar memories of the childhood abuse. If you were her dentist and she finally managed to explain her tightly clenched jaws and white knuckles, how would you respond?

I was standing in line for Holy Communion in a Roman Catholic church where most of the communicants were older women accustomed to receiving the host on the tongue. I have difficulty enough with standing for communion as it is. (We Episcopalians usually kneel.) But a terrible fear came over me with the rhythm of one female after another approaching the man called "father" and obediently opening their mouths. When it came to my turn, I thrust out my hand and stuck the dry wafer in my mouth with no offer of consoling wine to wash it down. (We Episcopalians always communicate in both kinds.) I longed to stay after the Mass and tell the priest my plight. Could I tell you?

A certain lesbian marine is traveling from Washington D.C. to her base down South when she is mugged, robbed, and stripped of her clothes by a group of drunken college students returning from spring break. She is brought to the hospital where you work and keeps repeating, "It's just like when I was a kid!" You sense this is *not* the first time this has happened. How would you bind up the new wounds without addressing the old ones?

The stories are infinite—we have all survived *somehow* to this present time—and the masks of protection have done their work. But the flashbacks create a crack in these masks—and you, the zambuk, have caught a glimpse of the pain and suffering that lies beneath. *Do not run away in horror, please.*

I asked many survivors what response they want to their flashbacks, and they all said that respectful, nonjudgmental *listening* was the first requirement. I have experienced two forms of therapy myself: (1) the face-to-face "can I help you?" kind and (2) the analytic process of lying on a couch with my therapist behind me. I am not addressing professional therapists, but the listening mode suggested by these two forms is applicable for any pro-survivor.

At this time, any big commentary is not much use. A "Band-Aid" will at least stop the "bleeding." If the victim knows this is only the tip of the iceberg, and so do you, a sanctuary of some kind (not the "Titanic"!) is the kindest offer at the moment.

Did Jesus experience flashbacks? Undoubtedly, if he was human he had memories that were painful. Is it possible that Mary's listening at his feet (Luke 10: 38-42) was as much for him as for her? (I'd consider that the second kind of therapy). Martha's more confrontational listening (John 11:21-27) would suggest the first kind of therapy. What we do know is that their home at Bethany provided a safe haven where Jesus could go when he felt the need.

If a survivor calls you or lands on your doorstep with a painful memory, the space and privacy are most important. A pastor told me that he was trying to counsel a woman in the sacristy after my show, and eventually she broke down and said that the crucifix hanging on the wall in the sacristy was just like the one that hung above the bed as a child during her abuse. Not a safe place! I like the cool, clean, well-kept, beautiful room that my analyst provides in contrast to the awful clutter and disorder that I grew up with. You would never find a chair to sit down in my house as a child. There were always sweaters hanging over the backs and hoards of newspapers and old magazines. There was no space to just sit. The "where" is very important and so is the "when." As these efts appear so unexpectedly, you may receive a phone call at 3 a.m. or a house visit at 7 a.m. or a frantic confrontation just when you are about to serve dinner for six-teen people. Unlike the professional, you do not have office hours, and this particular "eft" may even push the person to suicide. How to respond?

Let me give an example. Just before Christmas, about six years ago, my parents were coming from England to visit. Advent had been extremely busy, and I was stressed out by trying to meet everyone's needs and expectations but my own. How to be a daughter when I felt I was crawling with efts? The house was untidy and dirty (just like the one I grew up in), and I was all alone with only a few hours to fix it all. I felt like doing what I often did as a little girl—running away from home. In fact, I got in the car and thought of just pointing in the direction of Route 80 (we live near the George Washington Bridge) and heading towards California. As with the little girl, just sitting allowed the panic to die down. Eventually, I got out of the car. I called a friend.

"What needs to be done?" she asked.

"Everything!" I gasped.

"Start with putting clean sheets on the bed. Put some house cleaning music on the radio, and do one room at a time. Call me each time you finish a room." By that evening when my parents emerged through customs, I knew I could make it, and the efts had slipped back into the pond for the time being.

As you see, my pro-survivor was very specific. The chaos that flashbacks create in our lives needs to be met with a framework that is ordinary, orderly, and simple. If your survivor spouse is suffering flashbacks, it is not a good time for a pregnancy or a change of careers or a move or anything "extraordinary." We are given the opportunity *right now,* even as you read this, to participate in DeCaussaude's "Sacrament of the present moment." What can the zambuk do to encourage the survivor to let go of the past and live in the "now"? Reason is *not* helpful: "That was a long time ago; put it all behind you," is cruel and stupid (especially stupid). The feelings we have, we have, and even if you could weave a storyteller's spell, as Jesus did on the road to

Emmaus when the two disciples were coping with fresh, raw memories (Luke 24:13-35), what happens when you leave?

The two disciples, Cleopas and "the other" (I like to think it was his wife, Jesus's aunt, who was at the foot of the cross), invite Jesus to dinner and "he becomes known to them in the breaking of the bread." They see a glimpse of who he is, and so who they are. Transformation takes place. Instead of huddling together in pain, they return joyfully to the other disciples in Jerusalem all because of a simple everyday act. A discipline that meets the daily needs of your survivor is essential during this time. If frequent Communion is helpful, maybe you could offer to get up early and go with them—or a routine of regular Bible study or meditation or whatever brings the survivor back on track. If church is part of the problem, not the salve, you may have to be creative. Offer to drive them to therapy or Weight-Watchers or shopping or...? If the flashbacks seem serious enough to cause real concern about suicide, please make sure you have some professional help, especially if the person is not in therapy or unhappy with their therapist.

Before we move on to "adders," I would like to discuss "flash-*forwards*": our temptations and fantasies. They plague us all, and hours, weeks, months, years can be spent in daydreaming that stems directly from the childhood abuse we suffered. I believe that for category two and category three many of these fantasies will be sexual in nature. As with our night dreams, these all have messages for us and surely include our temptations. How can "we scatter the imaginations of the heart," as the Magnificat counsels us to do? Why does the average person, survivor or not, spend so much time in this futile occupation? Our sexual fantasies are based on the longing for rather than the actual attainment; the promise, not the fulfillment. For me these always seem more acute when I am needy, like after a performance when there is a terrible emptiness, a huge space that longs to be filled, a loneliness. A Native American story describing sexual intercourse says about orgasm: "and for a moment it took away the loneliness, almost, but not quite." This is the reality of the situation; no one and nobody could ever fulfill all our fantasies! St. Augustine (who must surely have been plagued with flash-forwards!) writes: "Our hearts are restless till they rest in thee." When I spoke to category one survivors, they at first denied that they ever had such fantasies. But in probing, I found that in fact they did; power and revenge featured heavily in their temptation. St. Paul seems to let his weakness in this area slip out from time to time: a nasty little comment about letting the knife slip for those who are so intent on circumcision before Baptism! Mean thoughts about "Alexander, the coppersmith" etc.!

Here we do well to consider what Jesus *did,* rather than quoting what St. Paul *said.* When Jesus emerged from his temptations in the wilderness, he confided these most awful secrets of his heart to *someone,* or we should not know the story today. In Gethsemani, he cried out in his loneliness that he needed someone to watch with him in the midst of his fears that "the cup" would be unbearable. In reality we know that he did not succumb to the temptations the devil offered him in the desert. In reality, he was brave and bore the cross even in the midst of that cry of desolation and loneliness: "My God, why has thou forsaken me?" Jesus did not repress any of this, nor should we. Perhaps because our fantasy lives are so intimate, we are reluctant to share them, especially with those who are close to us: "If I tell you who I really am, will you still love me?"

Yet if we can share our fantasies with another, how much better it is. Those who make and traffic in pornographic films and literature (especially child pornography) are propagating their own lust in very unhealthy ways, and those who watch it are so much in need of compassion and understanding to bring them into real life. Rock music is full of longings and fantasies of an adolescent nature. What are we to do with all these "passions," the need to feel good (or at least better)?

All of the synoptic Gospels tell us that after Jesus came out of the desert, he got on with the business at hand. Not that this was the end of all the temptations, "for the devil departed, biding his time." Lent can occur at any time for us, and flashbacks will pull us into a Lenten-feeling in the midst of August or on a fine fall day. However, my experience is that once we have emerged from "the desert" and the efts have slipped back into the pond, we need to move on. It is an easy stage to be stuck in and many survivors do that. They must drag up every last eft from the pond—then what? One's whole life can be governed by flashbacks and flash-forwards so there is nowhere to go. I think we do need a firm hand to help us out of this dilemma. Many survivors seem incapable of helping themselves and will often appear like little boys and girls. At an extreme, I encountered a woman of forty-five who reverted to a three-year-old—a large lady lying on the floor whimpering, "Daddy, don't do it to me!"—her flashbacks so complete that she was reliving the situation of her abuse right before my eyes. This lasted for as long as fifteen minutes while I just knelt beside her, praying for the Holy Spirit to give me a means to help her out of her pain. At last I said, "I hear you have a daughter of seventeen. So do I." (I had overheard her at lunch discussing her daughter.) There was no response, but she did hear me. Then I said, "I'm forty-seven." In a little girl's voice she said, "I'm forty-five." Gradually, with more talk about daughters and middle age, I brought her back to the present. She sat up and cried in my arms. I felt very blessed, very exhausted, and, as she left, I had the feeling that something had been healed. (I hesitate to use the word exorcised.) The woman thanked me and said she felt a lot better. As for me, I went home and plunked myself in front of the most inane TV comedy I have ever watched, and it was wonderful!

A word of caution about attending support groups during this time. Your survivor will hear a great many powerful efts, and this may well be wrong for him or her. We cannot help but compare our pain, and sometimes this induces needless guilt. (Why am I complaining when this poor man suffered so much more than I did?) I also feel that this can make a person feel helpless: "My whole life is incest!" wailed one survivor. This is recycling the pain. Better to make a batch of cookies and deliver them to a nursing home or take a long walk in the woods or play the piano or swim ten lengths of the local pool or sit in front of the computer. At this stage you may well find the victim will return to the means they used as a child to survive. "What made you feel better about yourself after that happened?" you might ask. "Eating the entire contents of the cookie jar!" could be a response. "All right, let's do it!" you say. At least, you might see her smile.

"Do this in memory of me," Jesus told us. How do we transform painful memories into thanksgiving? How did the disciples on the road to Emmaus, with the memories of Jesus's torture and abuse still so alive within them, break bread without the searing pain of those terrible moments returning in technicolor to invade their psyches? They sat down to an ordinary evening meal and their hearts burned with the *good* memories of that walk, that supper, and they knew Resurrection.

In her book, *Moments of Being,* Virginia Woolf records many memories from her childhood, including one of being held on a shelf and sexually abused by her half-brother, Gerald. She says, "I still recall it vividly," and yet this brave little girl could pull up her Victorian panties and forget it all in reading and writing. She wrote her first novel at the age of ten. In this same book she also recalls a moment of ecstasy from very early childhood (a moment of "Being") as she lay in bed in the nursery at St. Ives, Cornwall, and listened to the sea and the wind. Along with painful memories, I believe all of us have "moments of Being" like this. Mine are associated with the theater and also with the *good* things about my childhood and my mother and father.

At the end of her excellent book, *Reclaiming Our Lives,* Carol Poston mentions that her abusive father, whom we have come to know and despise, was also the one who coached his daughter to win the spelling bee for the whole state and shed tears of joy when she told him of her victory. The disclosure comes as a shock. I understand that Carol could not have brought that good memory into the first few chapters of her book. We, the readers (survivors), need the clear, clean sword of our hatred before we can accept the complexity of the issue. However, the pro-survivor needs to have a relative view of the abuser, and while it is of utmost importance that you believe the horrible things you are hearing, you should keep a distance from the story, and know in your heart that there may be a time when the survivor can see his or her way clear to a more balanced view of the past (around the time of the toads). You cannot hurry the process any more than you can hurry a nine-month pregnancy. The eft stage is hope newly conceived.

I have found powerful friends in the communion of saints as I listen to the "efts" of my fellow survivors. I pray for the help of a St. Teresa of Avila, who gives us a very telling story of her childhood in her *Life* and who could write at the end:

> Let nothing disturb you,
> Nothing cause you to fear.
> All things pass away,
> God remains ever the same.
> Patience gains everything.
> Whoever has God needs nothing else.
> God alone is sufficient.

St. Paul's "Whatsoever things are pure, whatsoever things are lovely, whatsoever things are of good report, think on these things" is also something every zambuk needs to hear. A nurse in an emergency room at an inner-city hospital told me that in a lull she looks out of the window and the tree outside refreshes her.

At such times, to read of modern-day celebrants such as Elie Wiesel and Viktor Frankl, who survived the most terrible abuse imaginable during the Second World War, is truly inspirational, for at this stage you may want to give up on your friend (and the whole world).

> "Hold me fast, don't let me pass,
> I am your baby's father," cries Tam Lin.

Keep the New Life, "the baby," always before you.

hold me fast
don't let me pass

II THE ADDER:

TOXIC GUILT AND SHAME

What happens to Janet as she is holding the little slippery eft and finds instead that she is clasping a poisonous snake? Can she hold up the adder, triumphant as a Minoan goddess, seemingly poised to dance away? Or tame the serpent, as the ancient German legends of St. Martha suggest? Or should she crush the adder underfoot quite firmly and impersonally, as we see in the statues of the Virgin Mary? Or, armed with lance and spear, attack the serpent straight in the mouth, like St. George in the icons of the Greek and Russian Orthodox Church? How do we handle times when one fragment of our lives is dropping away and another is poised to take its place?

As anyone knows who has given birth, transition is the most painful part of delivery. Your whole body seems stretched and focused on the new emerging life. Let us examine two possible scenarios:

The typical American hospital delivery in the 1950s

The mother has consulted no Wise Woman and is truly ignorant of the miracle that is taking place within her own body. The father is frightened and anxious, pacing the halls, as removed from Tam Lin's impassioned and repeated cry: "I am your baby's father!" as night and day. On the day of delivery (the Birth-Day), the "patient" is comatose; the all-powerful doctors and nurses swathed in robes and masks are dripping with anesthetics. Forceps, bright neon lights, shining steel bowls, a shaved vulva, an episiotomy, rubber gloves, harsh words, and a slap on the bottom all greet the emerging child.

Natural home delivery

Contrast the delivery room with a natural home delivery in a quiet, clean bedroom, perhaps with an apple tree in blossom outside the window. The good midwife and loving, supportive father are squatting in front of the mother, smiling in encouragement and pride. My friend gave birth in this second way, and, at the time of transition, as she was locked in the arms of her husband, forehead to forehead, they both breathed and relaxed, contracted and released, as the midwife directed. At the very moment when the baby's head crowned, the midwife, on the sidelines of this magnificent and ordinary drama, was there to catch the baby. The mother than presented the baby to the father on her knees. The midwife tied the knots in the umbilical cord and handed the father the scissors. After the cord was cut and the placenta delivered, mother and baby were gently bathed and readied for the first breast-feeding. This is probably the kind of birthing process that took place in Bethlehem nearly 2,000 years ago.

Many fathers, like mine, were absent or banished from the birthing process from the 1940s through 1970s. This divorces sensual pleasure from the mystery and pain of reproduction. The father who assists at a birth, in the way described above, is less likely to see his child as a plaything, an object. The mother who feels praised and prized for her hard labor, first hand, can connect naturally as parent and child. A little boy in a class I taught in Scotland, whose mother was breast-feeding his baby sister, said to me thoughtfully, pointing to my breasts, "You've never used those things, have you?" His words ring in my ears as a great truth. We had a situation in the 1950s where women's breasts, as Jayne Mansfield and Marilyn Monroe reminded us, were for men's pleasure and *not* baby's nourishment. This all added up to a climate in which covert and overt incest could flourish unde- tected. These are the adult survivors now pounding on the doors of therapists and counselors. I am one of them, and I still live with the confused messages I received about birth and sexuality as a child. There is a deep regret and a lot of resentment for the way I unknowingly participated in the bad birthing system with my own children. If I had to do it again...but now it is too late.

We are a society living with postpartum blues, postpartum tremors, and we are still so groggy from the anesthetics that the memories are only of the pain and horror and not of the good news that new life is at hand. We are only just taking the lid off all of the abuse—only a crack. Transition is the first thing that catches the eye.

The work of the zambuk during the time of transition is very similar to that of the good midwife. Yet many victims of child- hood abuse will tell of therapists and "friends" who tried to drug them with mind-numbing, dangerous drugs when flashbacks were terrible. These actions will have left the abuse victims feeling powerless and victimized over and over again by the very process that was supposed to heal! *You cannot dull the pain of transition artificially.* It is the rare birth that needs the intervention of hos- pital and drugs. This is *good* pain, for it leads to new life. Just as Jesus' pain on the cross was short-lived, we, at the foot of the "cross" for the survivor, must stay and pray. That is all we can do. In the second scenario, we are in the place of the midwife, not Tam Lin, the baby's father. A huge mistake that many well-mean- ing pro-survivors will make is to try to take away the pain.

The summer my mother died, I returned from the funeral in England (where my father had courageously revealed much of *his* childhood pain on the night of the funeral) and immediately fell down a flight of stone steps. Even as I fell, I knew that God was doing this for me. Muscle spasms are about as painful as labor pains, and the "lying in" that was forced upon me by the back injury all through that long, hot, humid summer was a time of tremendous emotional and spiritual rebirthing. After one particularly painful spasm, I remember the connectedness I felt with all who were being tortured at that very moment all over the world. Now I *knew* why Jesus had submitted to scourging and the crown of thorns. I knew it, not just in my imagination but in the reality of my own body! "Pain is a holy angel," said Dietrich Bonhoeffer from the depths of Tegel Prison. To recognize that this is a dark angel but not a demon is essential for the pro-survivor. The worst response for me during the summer of 1987 came from those who, in a sense, wanted to knock me out cold, wake me up when it was all over (after they had done the delivering!), and say, "Mrs. Nobleman, it's a boy!"

The good mother and father stay focused and attentive to all the pressures, the sensations, the miracle of this transition time and allow the Holy Spirit to work it through. The good midwife will be there to say "Push!" or "Don't push!" and to encourage ("You are doing so well!" "That hurts, I know, but I am so proud of you!") and, if necessary, to call for the ambulance if some kind of outside intervention is needed. For thousands of years, millions of adult survivors of childhood abuse have had to rely on shamans and grandmothers, kind friends and strange Samaritans to help them onto the journey to wholeness. It is twentieth century hubris to think that we know better. The good Samaritan did not stop to consult his first-aid book before binding all the wounds of the traveler. He used what he had available, and, it seems, a good deal of common sense. We could all do worse. Without the Jewish midwives, the great hero, Moses, would not have survived his "child abuse"! To be a midwife is honorable work.

You may be thinking that giving birth to an adder is not going to do anyone much good! However, the only other alternative is to be stuck in the eft stage when you know that Tam Lin, your True Self, is the end goal.

In many myths and fairy tales, the *perseverance* of the hero or heroine is the most important factor. Listen to Mozart's *The Magic Flute* and hear of the trials of Tamino and Pamina, of Papageno and Papagena. Or read of patient Penelope of ancient Greece, weaving and unweaving while her husband, Odysseus, sailed the seas on his hero's journey, or of Jacob who labored for seven years for the love of Rachel. And *take heart*. Holding the adder is only part of the process. We have nothing to fear from it, though a random sampling of everyone in your office or family would seem to say otherwise. I suppose the snake heads the list of most feared of all creatures—at least in Western society. Why is this so?

I took my nieces and nephews to the London Zoo last fall— all seven of them. It was interesting that the girls, Jessica and Elizabeth, were the ones who feared the snakes and had nightmares about them, while the boys, Jonathan, Daniel, Reuben, Benjamin, and Nicolas, were fascinated, especially by the tales of the venom of the serpent. We were all glad to come out of the reptile house into the sunlight, but the memories of the huge, coiled, green serpent or the little black and gold snakes are vivid for me to this day.

We have very confused feelings about snakes in the Western Hemisphere. On the one hand, we see them as loathsome creatures, cursed and horrid, cold-blooded, representing for both men and women a kind of phallic phobia. On the other hand, we are intrigued by this creature that sheds its skin and seems to respond to something deep within us—a wisdom. "Be ye wise as serpents," says Jesus, and the healing power of the snake is seen in the logos of many hospitals and other practitioners of the healing arts.

If we look a little closer at the fear of Phallus erect, we see clearly that this demon comes from the dark side of the imagination. In reality, Phallus is not normally erect but limp and harmless as a snake in its natural habitat. The sudden uncontrollable surge of blood into the penis, causing it to stand erect (like a snake raising its head), is a mystery that neither reason nor will can fathom.

Out of control and misused, as in child abuse, Phallus *is* terrifying. But those who wish to help the survivor will have to conquer this fear and see the reality. Many male child molesters are addicted to unnatural sexual intimacy and ruled by the Phallus god—irrational, uncaring, and all-consuming. Reason does *not* come into the picture. They cannot control themselves by an act of the will.

There is a complementary female fear associated with the snake who makes his home, his retreat, in a hole, the womb of the Earth. This, in Freud's term, is Vagina Dentata, the power of the female to suck in the male member, keep it captive, chew it up, and spit it out. It is associated with the Wicked Witch, who takes the symbol of hearth and home (the broom) and puts it between her legs (like Phallus erect) and flies through the night to do her evil. The nagging mother, the mean school teacher, the nasty old lady who lives in the haunted house, these are all Vagina Dentata, and she is feared by men and women alike. She may also be as seductive and sexually voracious as the male.

Yet, the truth is that without the *sometime* erect Phallus, we have no way of transferring New Life, and in reality, vaginas do not have teeth but provide a warm welcoming place to receive the sperm and deliver the child.

In preparing and presenting my one-woman show *Masks and Mirrors*, I have had to look very closely at the role of the abuser. When Julia Lee DeLisle, my professional mask-maker in London, and I sat down in a little restaurant in Wimbledon five years ago to work on creating a mask for the abuser to wear, she asked me, "How do you see him?" She sketched this picture on a napkin and it never changed. The resulting mask, from Julia's first impression, is the same. He wears a pair of red satin pants from the 1930s that belonged to my dad and were used in India in a play he wrote. (He played the devil and these were his pants!) The abuser's top is a plain black sports jacket. I stand on a table and have a person (who stands in for the child-victim) open up a big, brown doctor's bag and hand up various props that he uses. When I first started doing the show, I had cue cards that went with each prop to prompt the audience, but subsequent performances have shown me that the visual images are much

Julia Lee DeLisle's original drawing for the "Abuser" mask used in Roberta Nobleman's show *Masks and Mirrors*.

stronger than the words and need no explanation. The reaction when I turn around wearing the mask is almost palpable. In Rochester, a voice from the audience called out: "That's my father!"

It comes as a terrible shock for a young man to find out that his future father-in-law, a fellow he has grown to like and admire, has sexually abused his bride-to-be as a child. Or for my brother, who all his life has put his father on a pedestal, to suddenly hear that same father has abused his sister, his nieces, and his cousins. Or for a spiritual director, a woman of great integrity and chastity, to learn that the pastor she sees every day is the same man accused of abusing the altar boys in her CCD classes.

In considering the response to the perpetrator, let me say clearly that the adder stage is by far the most traumatic for everyone concerned. For the zambuk to feel pity, concern, even understanding at this stage is just too much to ask. When I first told my husband about Dad, his "I can't take this in," "This is so alien to me," "I can't believe it!" was very natural. He did something for himself which I believe was very healing for him. He got up and turned my father's photograph (a recent one, tacked up in the kitchen) to the wall. We turned it around only last year—a symbolic act.

I would like to take as a central parable for this chapter the Adam and Eve story. The snake (adder) features prominently in this story, which has endured over the centuries, precisely, I believe, because it deals with three very important aspects of our shared humanity: shame, blame and rejection.

"And the eyes of them both were opened, and they knew that they were naked, and they sewed fig leaves together and made themselves aprons." It is obvious to us twentieth century Westerners, and especially Christians, that the naked parts that caused Adam and Eve such shame were their genitals: the reproductive life-giving parts of themselves that hitherto, it seems, they had not known as shameful. Among "primitive" societies, nineteenth century missionaries commanded "the pagans" to "cover their shame." Is this a myth that only applies to a Judeo-Christian idea of sin and shame, or does it have a more universal appeal? St. Irenaeus believed that the principal wounding of Adam and Eve was in their sexuality. We have inherited—all of us—this loss of innocence. I believe that the primitive Adam and Eve might just as well have sewn aprons if the sin was child sexual abuse.

There is nothing more lovely than the joy that springs from the adult Adam in seeing the adult Eve: "Bone of my bone, flesh of my flesh! How like me, yet how delightful and wonderful the differences!" Suppose Adam were an adult, but Eve was a little girl. Lovely, yes, but how will this large organ fit into so small an opening? What of this little "curtain" that seems to cover the window to his joy? In our humanity—not in our culture or the time we were born—is the loud, clear voice of "Taboo!" where adult/child sexual intercourse is concerned. You, the zambuk, are going to hear voices that will say: "They have such child/adult intercourse on remote islands of the Pacific," or "In ancient Greece, man/boy 'love' was part of the culture." That does not make it right or good, and besides, we don't live on a remote island in the Pacific nor in ancient Greece. There is an innate feeling in the child: "This is bad touching!"

The picture of myself, at the age of eight, during the abuse, shows a little girl full of shame. I felt dirty and bad. This shame was reinforced at age nine because I developed a terrible abscess on the vulva. I have vivid memories of being taken to a fat, elderly doctor who blamed my mother for not keeping this child clean "down

The author at the age of eight.

there." I remember the shame I felt waiting in the doctor's office and trying to explain to the other little girls that, No, I didn't feel like skipping rope today...yet I could not say why. These abscesses, forty years later and after numerous recurrences, have created a sinus duct, which is *finally* being addressed in surgery, but this time with a kind and listening female doctor from the Philippines, a true Good Samaritan to me. That this shame should have lasted through the births of three children and over forty years is not unusual. My obstetrician was a man not unlike the doctor of my childhood. There was no way I could have told him about the abscesses when they occurred. I merely doctored myself and put up with the discomfort. The relief I felt when I was able, at last, to tell my story to Dr. Fe, my current gynecologist, was enormous. Shame is a very toxic burden. Again, in intimate personal matters, a person of the same sex is often the best *first* confidante.

We are told that the woman in the Gospels with the issue of blood, who for twelve years dragged her shameful anemic body from doctor to doctor (were all of them male?), spent all that she had. She finally found the courage to approach the real source of all healing: Christ. "Someone told her about Jesus," the Gospels tell us. That "someone" (another woman?) was a true zambuk, and the time was ripe. Encouraged, I believe, by this one who knew Jesus (Was it Mary?), she pushes her way through the crowd to touch the hem of his garment. Now comes a most significant part of the story for all of us with a shame-filled history: Jesus stops and says, "Who touched me?" Pragmatic Peter explodes, "Master, the crowds are hemming us in on either side and you say who *touched* me?" Jesus is talking about a very different kind of touching. Down through the ages, people have claimed to be touching Jesus when, in effect, like Peter and the crowd, they are merely touching each other, not the Christ. Jesus looks all about him. The woman, seeing she has been detected (Was it those tell-tale bloody stains on her dress?), comes trembling and falls on her knees in front of Jesus and explains *in front of everyone* (Peter, all those male disciples, Jairus, his servants—all strangers) "how it had been with her" (twelve years of pain and suffering to sum up in a few moments, in front of a hostile, impatient crowd—how could she do it?) "and how when she had just touched him, she had been immediately cured."

I know the feeling, Flo. (I call her Flo, this nameless woman.) When I told my abscess story to Dr. Fe, I felt empowered too. Jesus felt the power going out of him to her. A miracle that shame revealed in the presence of Christ can work in all of us! In the original Greek, the word *crowd* is used twice in this story. The first time *before* the woman is healed, when, indeed, they are just a mob of people, and the second time after her healing and public "showing" takes place. The second word should be something like *community*. This woman's story has touched a common chord within the bloody issues of all of these people. Did Peter think of Flo when he wept for shame and, more to the point, told someone about his weeping after he had denied his Lord three times? Thank you, Flo. Without your courage would I have been able to write these last few paragraphs, except that I know that in the "community" out there we all have our "bloody issues," our shameful secrets? The "going in peace" that Jesus confers on Flo is not an immediate serenity, but a dropping of the adder into its safe place and a transition to the next stage of the journey. "Your faith has healed you," says Jesus. Overhearing these words at the back of the crowd is the zambuk, the one who told her about Jesus. How do you feel?

If you have picked up this book, you are probably aware of the many books on shame and guilt that are to be found on the shelves these days. This can be most confusing. A husband of a survivor went to a weekend workshop on shame with his wife and ended up having to listen to a shocking story of serial rape by a crying woman who left him feeling guilty and helpless over the mere fact of being male! This workshop was led by a leading authority on shame in psychology today. The couple came to a retreat that I led, hoping it would help them recover from that workshop on shame! I have also heard many pro-survivors declare that they feel humiliated and ashamed being made to listen to story after story of incest.

If you are a left-brained kind of person, then all these books on shame and guilt and the differences between unhealthy and wholesome shame, good and bad guilt, will be helpful in your understanding. This much you do know: Your survivor certainly felt shame over what happened to them as a child. Even a modern-day star who comes out and proclaims on all the tabloid magazines at the supermarket check-out counter "I am a victim of incest!" by page three of the story will confess that this is not something she or he is proud of. We may be proud of ourselves that we have survived through the pain and had the faith to expose ourselves publicly, but we are not proud of the act of incest itself—of that we remain deeply ashamed, at least at this stage in the process. Personally, I was deeply ashamed, and for years I could not bring myself to even mention the word "incest." I was not just ashamed of myself but also ashamed of my dad (this was *so* difficult because, in many other ways, I was proud of my father) and our whole family. When I came out into the open and confessed my horrible secret, I had the sense that somehow I had let down the family name, even my church, even the country of my birth! When an Italian woman once said to me that she thought there was more child sexual abuse in England than in Italy because the English were so cold and undemonstrative and had a tendency towards homosexuality that was not so prevalent among passionate, unrepressed Italians, I found myself rushing to the defense of my country!

If we return to the three houses of Chapter II, we see that all three were shame-based, in one way or the other. In house number one, the victims see themselves as being guilty of sin—sex being the worst sin. Virginia Woolf describes this as "looking-glass shame" and goes on to say that she was ashamed of her own body because of her childhood abuse. This carried over into her adult life, so she could not ever enter a room in a new dress or powder her nose in public without an intense sense of shame. Many adult survivors feel this way about their bodies—and particularly do they hate and abhor their genitals.

In my case, as a number two home dweller, I have never felt ashamed of my body. I am at home with my body and I believe this is due to the way in which I dealt with the shame as a child. While other children may have blanked out, paralyzed themselves as with an anesthetic during the abuse, I simply pretended I was someone else: my shame was in my *mind*. When my beloved maternal grandmother died when I was eleven, I remember feeling real grief *at first*, but then I caught sight of my crying face in the mirror and immediately my tears ceased as I contemplated the tragic face that would be so wonderful in a future theatrical play!

I think this is a paradigm for many number two survivors. Prostitutes will tell you that they separate themselves from the shame-filled act—it's almost schizophrenic. My own shame was, and is, directly related to the abuse, but more in my psyche than my body. That I suddenly, at age seven, dropped in class from being twelfth to being thirty-ninth was shameful to me. That I developed terrible carelessness about my personal property (I was scared to go home one day because I had lost my ninth pair of gloves that winter!)—that was shameful. I remember an encounter between Mr. Spare, the teacher when I was nine years old, and my mother when he showed her my inky, dirty, blotched work. These were the days of dip pens. I was ink monitor, and I hated the job of filling up the ink wells in the desks. I *always* spilled some and was left with shameful hands—covered in black ink, the nails torn and bitten. Great hands for playing the wicked witch, but I would never be cast as the fairy princess! My mother protested that the work was imaginative and well-written, but Mr. Spare marked it "F" all the same. With the BBC 1940s radio broadcasts of "Music and Movement for Schools with Ann Driver," I could lose myself, body and soul, in the marvelous world of creative drama. Thank you, Ann Driver. You will never know what you did for me!

A young boy already knows that he is "different" from the other boys at school when he hears a gang in the boys' washroom bragging about conquests with girls that seem totally alien to him. He is in love with the male art teacher and has no young-boys-network to share his feelings. Imagine a young girl strongly attracted to the older camp counselor, yet knowing she must return home to the furtive fumblings and abusive attention of her older brother. The recent hypocrisy over accepting gays in the military sends a powerful message: "Stay inside your closet—ashamed—and we will tolerate you. But who you truly are is not acceptable to us."

How did God respond to Adam and Eve's shame? How did Jesus answer the woman's shame in the story of adultery? (John 8). We overlook the many incidents of God our Mother in the Bible, and surely the image of God "making coats of skins and clothing the shame of Adam and Eve" is a motherly action, even if it is the "Lord God" who does this. If we look at Jesus and the woman caught in adultery, he will not shame her as those who brought her to him have already done. In fact, he averts his eyes from her as he draws in the dust in the ground and only confronts her when her accusers have already left—perhaps in guilt themselves after hearing "Whoever is without sin cast the first stone." Beginning with the oldest, they leave. Does that say that wholesome guilt is more easily recognized the longer we live in this world?

How to administer comfort to those who may be filled with a toxic shame that is imprisoning their whole life? Julian of Norwich, that wise and wonderful woman, has much to say about sin. Some people consider her views of the "Godly will within us all that never assents to sin" to be at best naive and at worst heretical. However, I feel Julian has formulated this comfortable doctrine out of her own pain and shame. Julian had a vision at the age of thirty-and-a-half and, it seems, wrote down the first shorter version of her "showings" soon afterwards. The longer version written many years later, after time for much spiritual growth, lacks all the self-deprecating remarks of the first version ("I am only a woman"…"unlettered"…"this sinful creature," etc.) and develops a lovely, peace-filled view of a world where even our bowel movements (something we are often taught to be ashamed of!) are "God's action, when the body opens and closes in seemly fashion, like a purse"! If we are to believe that Jesus took upon himself all of our shame in the action of the cross, then this is True Wisdom. We are enfolded in love—as the Genesis story puts it, wrapped in God's well-tailored coats.

My zambuks have helped me to locate the shame in my *mind* and accept that the ways I used as a child—and still use—to cover my shame (my fig leaves) served me well…until they wear out. In the book (and movie) *The Prince of Tides*, the narrator Tom (abused most brutally as a child) develops in his mind an image of the misunderstood Southern Gentleman—the coach whose team has "gotta win." But the giant-size chip on his shoulder—bigger than a defensive player's shoulder pads—is eventually removed, painfully and slowly, through the power of love and forgiveness.

My shame as an adult comes in the form of negative voices:

"You are not worth a standing ovation." "You are not a nice wife or a good mother." "In fact, you have it all wrong, dear, because you, at heart, *are* a hussy, a slut, a mess." When you hear totally peaceful, humble persons, like the Dalai Lama or Marian Anderson, you sense that through prayer and meditation they have discarded the fig leaves that separate them from God and from us. There is a transparent quality about them. They could not care a fig if ten-thousand people or two turn up to hear them speak. (If the DAR does not want Marian Anderson, the great African-American contralto, in Constitution Hall in 1939, that is their problem, not hers.) They are not ashamed.

The bodily shame of number one survivors manifests itself in trembling fear on the massage table or analytical couch, in a refusal to swim on a hot day because they can't bear to put on a swimsuit, and in a hundred other shame-based messages that began in childhood.

I met the most marvelous, whole, funny, warm, big-hearted priest in Australia. I don't know if he had ever experienced any number three horrors, but he definitely seemed to be free of the closet and sunned himself by the Lake of Beauty. He filled his church and rectory with the most gorgeous paintings, music, and theater. Because he was totally accepting of who he was, he could respond to my neediness by simply filling up the gaps that my shame sometimes gouges in my psyche. He did so with charm, lightness, good humor, and just plain fun. In his back garden, my friend had a dead gnome—a little blue-trousered statuette sprawled over a low wall with a dagger in his back! Australians, like the English, can be very "cute" with their gardens and ornaments. (Another word for it is "bad taste"!) When I feel downcast in shame, I think of the dead gnome in Australia and start to laugh. I left behind a resurrected gnome, complete with little lantern, for my friend to be opened on Easter Sunday.

A fellow number two home dweller constantly dreamt of knives stuck in his chest or stomach. I still have a piece of art therapy he did that does *not* bring a smile. Encounters with well-meaning zambuks had only helped turn the knife and embedded it deeper into his flesh. Gently withdrawing that knife, looking into the wound, cleansing, and suturing required long-term convalescence in a safe and loving environment where he could find the nurturing he desperately needed. His alcoholic father was part of the problem, but the most damage was done by sleeping with his mother until the age of nine. There were sisters and brothers in this family, but only the boys got to sleep in Mommy's bed! Unconsciously, he had been seeking those warm soft breasts, that closeness, in all the wrong places. Dearest friend, *you* were not to blame as a child, as a man, but it had to be attended to by professionals—for that was incest.

What of the fig leaves the pro-survivors themselves may be wearing? What if the reflection in the mirror is your own shame? This might be worth a dusting off for both of you. The sharing that Adam and Eve could do for one another *after* the Fall was surely healing. The least we can do is assure ourselves that God does not hate what God has made.

Does this include the perpetrator too? As the Quakers say, "A light within *all* of God's creatures"? Is there a "Godly will" within him or her that "never assented to sin"? Jesus speaks of a sin against the Holy Spirit which does seem to be beyond God's saving grace. Especially at this traumatic stage, when all of life seems colored by the devastating news you have just received like a blow on the head, the person who needs the pity, the enfolding love of God, most of all is probably you, the pro-survivor. A person in shock needs to realize that it cannot be "business as usual." How do you respond when the abuser (your future father-in-law) suddenly calls to check on the details for the wedding rehearsal? Or good old Dad, the perpetrator, drops by and wants to dandle your daughter on his knee? Or Father, the pedophile, is the celebrant at the Mass you are attending? You can see only *the abuser* at this stage—to expect anything more is unreasonable. A friend and her husband came to visit me in England when I was visiting my dad and he was sick. My friend had known my story for years and felt real pity for Dad and conversed with him in a warm and intimate way. Her husband had only recently heard the whole story, and he sat ramrod straight and poker-faced on a chair the furthest away from Dad. He afterwards confessed to his wife that all he could see was this *abuser* and he couldn't make civil conversation. He kept his distance like a man with a poisonous snake!

So what distances can you create for your own comfort zone and protection at this stage? It is a very important question and one you might want to share with a wise neutral outsider (but not your survivor). When you are ready, you may come closer. After performing my show on child abuse for inmates of Rahway Prison at the Adult Diagnostic and Treatment Center—a branch that serves over seven hundred child molesters, rapists, pedophiles—I was most touched by several prisoners who came to me afterwards to thank me for coming to perform for "me, a child molester" or "me, a serial rapist." I interrupted this palpable shame and asked their names: "Paul," "Ed Joe," "John." "That's who you are to me," I said. God calls us by name. During this very fragile time maybe the best we can do for ourselves is to repeat our names and some day we may be able to say theirs too, without choking.

What can enforce the toxic shame? I was speaking with a monk one day. When I reached the word "incest," he got up and closed the door. When I questioned him, I found this was not to ensure greater privacy for me but that truly he was ashamed of the subject matter. Further questioning revealed many unsolved, raw, bloody issues within his own childhood. Several times, I have felt guilty because I have spoken an extra ten minutes about incest in a room full of people where I know there was just one survivor out there who needed to hear what I had to say. You, the zambuk, may often feel exasperated and impatient with your survivor, the abuser, and yourself. I have often caught myself thinking, "Why am I taking up this healthy person's time and energy with my sickening story?"

Only God's infinite patience and tenderness can help us deal with dreadful demon number two: blame. We know that Adam and Eve's sin manifested itself in blame. By the age of two, whenever we are able to communicate, we have already learned this awful art to a fine degree. Said my two-year-old son, after picking off all the heads of the flowers in the garden, "Celia made me do it." "But your sister is in school!" "All the same, she made me do it!" was the reply, with a look on his face as ancient as Adam's! Without good enough parenting, this sets up a deadly pattern in our lives that causes a rift between us and our Maker. Eve blames the serpent; Adam blames Eve; God curses the serpent; the vicious cycle is set up. Some blame God for putting a temptation like the Tree of Knowledge of Good and Evil in the way of Adam and Eve and then forbidding us to eat from it. We all know forbidden fruit tastes better! That is one of the reasons for the wide-spread perpetuation of incest.

Imagine a man like my dad, accustomed to a life of adventure, violence, and power as a regimental sergeant major in the Army, living in the excitement of the jungles of India, Madagascar, and Africa during the war, returning home to a very dull routine as a petty business man managing his father-in-law's corner shop. There was a pregnant wife, who had lost an interest in sex and replaced it with the all-absorbing business of motherhood. And here, ready and available, was this attractive little girl with the black curls, so much like him in temperament, so alluring and—forbidden fruit! Who could blame him?

Many victims report that the perpetrator blamed them for the abuse: "She wanted it as much as I did!" "Ann was so well-developed for a thirteen-year-old." "He had an erection the moment I touched him." "I think we are dealing with a very seductive young lady," said the judge in a court case involving a five-year-old child and her uncle! Not only does the perpetrator blame the victim, so does society, and, often, so does the church. From St. Paul (1 Corinthians 11:3-16) to the twentieth century bishop or pastor, women and children have often been seen as seductive.

The Old Testament is full of such stories. What are we to do with "The Song of Songs"? "We have a little sister, and she hath no breasts: what shall we do for our sister in the day when she shall be spoken for?" There is a delightfully erotic innocence with children. This has been violated over and over again by adults. And even when this is not overt abuse, it has often been difficult for a man to know what to do with the feelings he has when he holds his little daughter on his lap. Or (something not spoken of so often) for a mother to know what to do with the excitement she feels as her little boy pulls at her nipple or toddles up and rests his head between her legs. I believe there is so much covert incest about that, that even if we wanted to, there is no way we can "stamp it out." In the adult survivor, vague memories emerge in the middle of life, confusing feelings about Uncle So-and-So when he visited at Christmas and played such marvelous, exciting games. Or a man who shamefacedly admitted that his mother's secret thrill when he came in from school (from kindergarten up till the age of seven) was for him to creep into her bed where she and the new baby were taking a nap and unbutton her blouse for his own refreshment. "Ever since then, I've been a breast man," he said. "And I married a flat-chested woman!"

Covert incest, I believe, can lead us into a heap of troubles precisely because it is all so vague and cloudy, and the mixed messages are many. How can we respond? One very clear thing needs to be said to the survivor—repeatedly, loudly, and with great conviction: *You were not to blame.* I assure you (even if she denies it), your survivor in some ways blames herself. The terrible responsibility we assume at such an early age grows heavier and heavier the older we become. There is no way that I could not have felt some blame towards myself as a child. Later on in life, we may in anger then turn the blame on "the other" (Adam-Eve) or the Serpent. Perhaps the one who assumes the greater part of the blame is God. I cannot tell you how many times I have heard Christians exclaim, "How could God allow such a terrible thing as child sexual abuse?" Yet, Jesus never blames anyone in any story in the Gospel as far as I can see. Not even Judas Iscariot. It's as though God says, "Here is this beautiful world with its amazing gift of the knowledge of Good Sexuality and Evil Sexuality [the "Tree"], and since you are bound to eat of this fruit and suffer the consequences, remember that I am the God who clothes you in my protection and love whenever you try to hide from me in shame and blame."

This non-blaming, neutral stance not only offers wisdom but also may lead us to look with God's pity on the whole sad situation. What does pity ask us to do? (Pity is different from mercy, which I believe comes at a later stage). If you and your survivor can begin to look with pity at least at yourselves, it may divert attention away from the "mea culpa" masochism that is so prevalent among survivors and pro-survivors alike. At this stage, to ask to pity anyone but yourself is too much, and even while you may rationalize in your head "I was not to blame," you may still feel in your gut "Wasn't there some way I could have stopped it?"

The zambuk may consider asking your survivor to show you a picture of themselves as a child. See if you can probe beyond "the mask" the little girl or boy probably put on to survive, to the reality. The interesting thing about that picture of myself at eight was that I was wearing no mask that day, no cover-up. My therapist had repeatedly asked me if I had any pictures of myself during the abuse. For two years I lied to her and said no. (I wasn't ready to deal with that picture then). I discovered it "by accident" and immediately my eyes filled with tears of pity. "It's true," I thought. "It really did happen. Poor little girl!" It was a real breakthrough of my denial.

One of the most prevalent ways that survivors mask the abuse as a child is through developing a false self, an extra skin like a snake. Here are some false selves that survivors use:

That Extra Good Little Girl or Boy: Mommy's Little Helper, Teacher's Pet, Father's Best Altar Boy, Grandma's Especially Good Girl. "If I keep quiet and good while he's beating brother Jim, maybe I won't get it too."

Top of the Class: "I may have this dirty little secret at home, but at school, see me shine!" "Books and tests, writing and reading, these can't hurt me!"

Everyone's Mother: *The Little Red Hen* or *The Giving Tree* is her favorite story. Often this mask is worn by the oldest in the family, like myself. I take care of everyone's needs (including my abuser's) except my own.

Everyone's Baby: This is often the youngest of the family. There is a learned helplessness, like that of the goddess Persephone in the Greek myth who, after being raped is sent into the underworld. "I'm a fragile little thing that needs Momma's (Demeter's) help all the way." She sucks her thumb, wets the bed, even reverts to baby-talk.

The Bad Girl or Boy: "You say I'm no good. All right, let me just show you how bad I can be!" This child seems to be acting "up" and "out" (but never "in"), calling out for attention. "See me!" the child seems to cry. "Notice me, please, somebody!"

I'm Nothing: This child wears an armor of protection to go with the mask. For example, this may be the fattest child in the family or class, the one with the glasses, the pimples, and very few friends. "Go away and leave me alone in my suffering" is the message they often give out.

I Don't Really Live on This Planet: This child is often termed "weird" by friends and family. To survive, the child learns to space-out, to live almost entirely in a world of fantasy. The child daydreams in class and wanders off into the country, as did Gustav Mahler (the great Austrian composer) as a little boy. Nature or music or outer-space or the world of fairy tale and legend seems to be the only "reality." The person wearing this mask is almost incapable of telling the truth; the lines are all blurred.

Anxious Annie/Troubled Ted: These anxiety-ridden children bite their nails, rock back and forth in their chair at school, love to hear tales of terror, are obsessed with "the shadow" side of life. They may develop all kinds of phobias or even an early addiction to something like alcohol just to deaden the pain of waiting for the next time "it" happens. By the time they get to high school, it's too late.

Runaway Robin: Found in fairy tales throughout the world, this child runs away from home. It's the only way out.

There are many, many masks—and some of us wear several.

Mine have been "The Bad Girl" and "Runaway Robin." Occasionally, I have succumbed to "The Little Red Hen"—my bad space in the Enneagram number two—but intrinsically the "Wicked Witch" despises being a "Goody-Two-Shoes!" I may be the one that always cleans the toilets in my house, but I do so in a careless slap-dash manner, complaining loudly.

What can the zambuk do to help us unmask?

I think the blame needs to be slowly replaced with accountability. A confessor once asked me what Jesus would have done if he had come up the stairs during the oral sex with my dad. I immediately began to make excuses for my father, to protect him from the blame. Father Andrew said, "I think Jesus would have kicked him downstairs! *You* haven't sexually abused your children." This helped me to place the blame squarely where it belonged: accountability.

Ultimately, the most helpful zambuks have been those who communicated to me that they loved me, masks and all. I can be "The Good Girl" *and* "The Bad Girl," "Stay-at-home Roberta" *and* "Runaway Robin."

What are we to do with the self-pity that can become a mask in itself? A most unattractive off-putting feature is "The Poor Little Me" attitude. In the theater, nothing alienates an audience so fast from a character as self-pity. What can lift the adult survivor out of the awful pit of self-pity and useless masochism? It is as if the survivor goes about wearing a "V" for victim on their chest. This learned victimization can be so insidious that it creates a terrible triangle: *victim—persecutor—rescuer.* If you, the pro-survivor, feel yourself slipping into any of these roles, move away very fast. To walk in someone else's shoes is not really possible. They won't fit your feet. Your "truth" cannot fix the problem any more than anyone else's; it will solve itself with the power of the Holy Spirit.

A teacher I know (a survivor) had a difficult class. One day, at the height of the chaos, she stood by wringing her hands helplessly, and a little girl came up to her and said, "You know what your trouble is, Miss? You're weak! Weak, weak, weak!!!" At that, the teacher burst into tears and ran to the faculty room. If you had been there, how could you have comforted her, moved her beyond that "hell" in which she was living?

Under these circumstances, there is often a snake-like tendency to crawl into a hole and retreat. The venomous tongue of the adder seems to have reached into the core of our being and can often drive us to despair, even thoughts of suicide. The rejection and subsequent *ejection* that Adam and Eve suffer as a result of eating the apple is very real. God's curse seems to ring in our ears: "Weak, weak, weak!" is what my friend heard. God, however, all along was saying, "You are my beloved daughter," and Jesus tells her, "I take this yoke of 'weakness' upon myself," and the Holy Spirit offers, "I will be your Advocate, your comforter." In actual fact, my friend realized that teaching was not for her and went on to find and prove her real strength in other ways. The little girl's rejection was in effect a "necessary death," painful as it may have appeared at the time.

I do very badly with rejection myself, and when that happens, I reach for one of my old survivor masks for protection without a second thought—or I used to.

Let me tell you the tale of Gethsemani Abbey—the actress and the monks. Back in 1986, I performed *Julian* for the Trappist monks in the small chapel beneath the visitor's balcony where women visitors were allowed. Two years later on a very hot summer afternoon, following a conference of all women and a retreat that I had led in nearby Nazareth, Kentucky (also for all women), I came to perform St. Luke's Gospel at Gethsemani and discovered that if I wanted space, I had to use the balcony above the little chapel. I could not use the main chapel. It all felt very familiar: Men, many of whom were called "father," were rejecting me, ejecting me from the one suitable good space to perform, and pushing me into another. It's as if a concert pianist were being asked to perform a Mozart sonata on a nasty little upright out-of-tune piano when down below was a beautiful concert grand. What would the true professional pianist do? (One without a history of rejection and ejection?) She would say, "Thanks for the invitation, but, no, I cannot play that piano. Good-bye!" Instead I, the victim, reverted to "little girl" behavior and lied, "Oh, that will be just fine! No, I don't mind doing it in the balcony. I can accommodate myself to you, Father." I gave a hurt, angry performance of the gospel according to Roberta! I abandoned the stories I had planned to do and replaced them with the story of the bent-over woman (Luke 13:10-17) plus a short homily for the monks on how Jesus had invited the woman into the men's part of the synagogue (unlike his twentieth century followers who had excluded me from their sanctuary!). Only very few monks attended this second performance, so I was feeling most unloved and unappreciated, and this manifested itself in bitterness and bad feelings. Yet, at that stage, I did not even realize I was angry. I just felt awful!

Of course, the few monks who did come responded in the way people always do when they are dumped upon: withdrawal and horror and avoidance. Who likes to be given a serpent when you were expecting a fish?

"East of Eden are the cherubim and a flaming sword which turned every way to guard the way to the Tree of Life" (Genesis 3:24). These littlest of angels and the magnificent sword of truth can bring Adam and Eve to an understanding that within the very act of rejection is life for the choosing. With grace, I have redeemed my "failure" at Gethsemani over and over again. God works in my weaknesses and makes them his strength. God our Mother has never truly rejected Adam and Eve. Or, as Julian would say, my sin at Gethsemani was "behovable." Somehow, given the pattern of my childhood abuse and the monks' history, it was a "necessary" part of my growth in understanding (and maybe theirs). Today, there is no way I would perform in a balcony; I have too much self-respect as an artist. And I understand there is no more women's balcony at Gethsemani Abbey. We have all grown and changed. The adder-like sting of rejection is only toxic if we don't pay attention to the wound. The zambuk may be the one who is called to suck out some of the poison and spit it out. Be careful not to swallow any of the adder's venom yourself! The monks at Gethsemani did well to recoil for a while and then reconsider what had caused this venomous-tongued woman. One of them at the time did come up to me and say he understood my hurt and anger. It was a learning experience for everyone. At this stage, you, the Good Samaritan, do not need to be cursed at by the wounded traveler when you are trying to bind the wounds. Understand, though, this cursing is not directed at you, the healer. Part of it may be for the assailants (the abusers), but a larger part is directed inward to the traveler himself: What a fool I was to take this journey from Jerusalem to Damascus.

Most important of all, *do not reject your wounded friend*. The bridegroom may not be able to look the abuser (his future father-in-law) straight in the eye, but he comforts the bride-to-be and assures her that, while he is in shock and does not understand, he accepts her and will come to accept the family some day.

After I told him of the abuse, my brother went for a three-hour drive alone round and round the Isle of Thanet in Kent (where my parents used to live), came back, and made the decision that he and his family would not be visiting for a while, but they would call.

Sister's presence at the Mass just may have been the one saving grace for the priest who had abused the altar boys. Anything more she can do for him and for the victims and their families will depend very much on her own spiritual health at the time.

Dealing with blame and shame and rejection needs all the grace available, and so I invite you to call on the Queen of Pity, Mary herself, who knows all about rejection and has always been there for the "little ones" of this earth in times of pain. If I have an understanding of what lies behind the Immaculate Conception of Mary, then she is there between the cherubim and the flaming sword and holding hands with Adam and Eve as they are driven from the garden, just as I see her walking down the temple steps after three sleepless nights and three anxiety-ridden days—Jesus, age twelve, on one hand, rejected Joseph ("Didn't you know I must be about my Father's business?") on the other. Mary is in our midst.

This most difficult of all chapters to write has left me exhausted, peevish, and frustrated. I feel rather like the Medusa who had all those snakes in her head (in our *minds* are where the adder stings are most poisonous). To rinse these adders out of our minds and stand ground very firmly to face the cruel bear is no easy task. Bears are bigger, but they are not all cruel. Buy yourself a teddy bear (or its equivalent comforter) before you read the next chapter! The midwife has left—now you need a pediatrician!

hold
me fast
don't let me
pass

III THE CRUEL BEAR:

THE ROLE OF SOCIETY, THE MOTHER, AND MOTHER CHURCH

E merging from the shame, the blame, and the rejection, looking horrified at the "V" for victim we are wearing and then around at the world we live in, is rather like a bear coming out of hibernation or a newborn leaving the hospital and coming home to bewildering new family life.

Who can help us through this new stage while we are still so dependent? In effect, we need now a kind of nursemaid or pediatrician. As Jesus looked out over Jerusalem, he longed to gather her people under his wings as a hen does her chicks. At this fragile stage, maybe you, the zambuk, need a "Mother Bear" yourself!

Bears are excellent mothers, highly protective of their young, attacking with raised paws any outsider, descending on the intruder in a very feminine way of fighting. Contrast the bull or stag, who attacks with horns, head on. The bears move slowly, ponderously, and often seem to avert their eyes to the ground. The well-ordered home of the three bears in the fairy tale provides a refuge for Goldilocks until they return home, and she flees in fear at those seemingly cruel bears.

Why do survivors choose teddy bears as the comforter of choice? I have yet to go to a survivor group or lead a retreat without at least one teddy bear in attendance (and occasionally there's one in the audience for a performance). What is it that makes a man or woman of forty-five carry about a teddy bear like Linus his blanket? I did a workshop using sock puppets at a church in New York City that had a recreation program for homeless people. I ended up giving away half of my sock puppets as these grown-up people held on to the puppets and couldn't bear to be parted from them! They had named them and were cuddling them in a way that brought tears to my eyes, perhaps for myself, as well as for them.

Roberta Nobleman at five months, with her mother and her father, who was on leave from the Army, in May 1942.

What is the role of the *good* bear? The uncruel one? The comforter? The Renaissance painters and Medieval sculptors present us with a very clear picture: the Universal Mother and the little helpless Child (the Presentation). The early bonding of mother and child is more important than many of us realize, and all those paintings of the doting Mother Mary with the six-week-old Jesus on her lap speak of a great truth: We all need a safe, warm, loving lap—especially at that beautiful age when the eyes have begun to focus, the mouth to smile in recognition, the ears to pick up familiar sounds, and the little hands to stretch out to feel the great and wonderful world.

What kind of lap did Mary provide for Jesus? Between the thighs is the softest, the most delicate flesh, and forty days after a birth, the bleeding has finally stopped, and, in Jewish tradition, Mary would have made her way to a special healing place for women, handed over the baby to someone else (Elizabeth?), and enjoyed those cool cleansing waters of purification. Surely a time of restoration, of prayer, and of sisterhood! The birthing place is somehow freed up, made ready for what the world has to offer. The pain, the tearing and bleeding of childbirth can be put aside, as the woman relaxes in the water and receives a little mothering herself.

The author with her son Paul, ten months old.

Breast-feeding is usually well established by then, and the mother begins to feel much more of a person in her own right. Perhaps Jesus had finally slept through the night, so Mary and Joseph could face the day with a little more equilibrium.

What if there is no wholesome lap to receive the little child? No place to dandle the little one on the knee? No strong, caring arms to support, to present the child to a hostile and difficult world? And what if the privilege is abused?

When I was a child, my mother gave me a New Testament with colored pictures. One of them showed Jesus with a little girl seated in his lap. Two years ago, I wrote under that picture: "Jesus with a little girl. He will not abuse her."

During the time when I was being sexually abused by my

father, an uncle of a school friend was visiting in a nearby house. I seem to remember they were poor people. It was a little crowded house with several children. The uncle was an older man and considered "good with children." He took me on his lap, pulled me against his now-hardened penis, put his hands into my vagina (little girls in the 1940s always wore dresses, never pants), and played with me.

He finally released me and we all went to play in the yard outside. After a little while, I climbed back on his lap for more. I seem to remember that we went to visit on several occasions while the uncle was there, and each time I went and sat on his lap. Now, forty-two years later, I understand why I did that.

Simeon prophesies to Mary at the presentation in the temple: "This child will be a sign that people will reject, and thus the secret thoughts of many will be laid bare." *Why the rejection? The denial? The avoidance?*

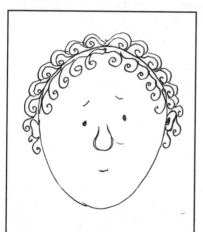

Julia Lee DeLisle's original drawing for the "Cleopatra" mask used in the show *Masks and Mirrors*.

Let us look a little closer at the cruel indifference of society, of Mother Church, and of the perpetrator's partner to the abuse. In Alcoholics Anonymous, this person is called the "enabler." In Jesus's parable, he would be the priest or Levite who passed by on the other side of the traveler. Here is the picture of the mask she wears in my show:

Her name is Cleopatra, Queen of Denial, and "De-Nial" is *not* a river in Egypt! It is the mark of the one who fails to protect the child when he/she is most vulnerable. Why does she do this when it seems so contrary to nature? The mother bear, the mother tiger, the guinea pig all protect their young—*unless* circumstances contrary to natural animal instincts call forth rejection. (e.g., mother guinea pigs in captivity often eat their young). My Cleopatra mask is worn above a vast heavy apron. It is the white net petticoat of a 1950s wedding gown—on one side, all pure and lovely, but on the other side: *a mess.* Let me describe some of its features: little brushes (for cleaning crumbs from the table); stain removal for clothes (Mama's washing is white and bright!); Mother's Day cards to the "Perfect Mom"; the little frilly apron of the good mother who stays at home to bake the cookies; the American flag (we are patriotic!); and pills—Mom is often a hypochondriac, totally absorbed in her own needs.

As Anita Hill revealed to us in the hearings for Clarence Thomas's nomination to the Supreme Court, racism may be part of it, too. I am a white woman, and I stand in deep respect and humility before the suffering of my brave sisters of African descent who in the past have borne a large share of child abuse and as adults have often been forced to deny their own motherly instincts and become "mammy" to the little white child.

A friend of mine (white) who grew up in the South says she is still dealing with guilt that her black nurse was made to breast-feed her first, and then the nurse's baby received the "left-overs." Breaking the silence of child abuse in black America has been the parable of Matthew 18:23-35 repeated over and over again. The fact that routine sexual abuse of child slaves by owners was then perpetuated by black men themselves onto their very own sets up a terrible chain of events. Black men too have often been humiliated—called "boy."

Incidents in the Life of a Slave Girl, written in 1861 by Harriet Jacobs under the pseudonym Linda Brent, tells a harrowing story of child sexual abuse: "My master began to whisper foul words in my ear. Young as I was, I could not remain ignorant of their import. I tried to treat them with indifference or contempt. The other slaves knew too well the guilty practices under that roof, and they were aware that to speak of them was an offense that never went unpunished. I longed for someone to confide in.

I would have given the world to have laid my head on my grand-mother's faithful bosom and have told her all my troubles. I dreaded the consequences of a violent outbreak, and both pride and fear kept me silent." Harriet continues: "I have concealed the names of places and given persons fictitious names. I had no motive for secrecy on my own, but I deemed it kind and considerate towards others to pursue this course."

Dearest Harriet, my sister, so did I. Fear kept us both in bondage. Can we lay blame to Harriet's grandmother, who probably knew what was going on because she herself had suffered likewise as a young girl? Can we blame my mother for so skillfully wearing that mask of denial over all those years? There is *no blame* intended here, and you, the zambuk, need to understand clearly why this partner operates the way he or she does.

What are the "props" Cleopatra might use for denial? *What does society do?*

Wear rose-colored spectacles: "We have the perfect family!"

Stick its head in the sand: "What you don't know won't hurt you!"

Sweep it under the rug: "Looks like a nice clean home."

Watch it on TV or read about it in the newspapers: "Isn't it a terrible world out there?"

Encourage it through Madison Avenue: Dress your little girls in enticing frilly panties and bikinis and give little boys guns and GI Joe toys for Christmas.

And what does society say?

"I just can't believe my ears!" "Liar!"

"Don't wash your dirty linen in public!"

"See no evil, hear no evil, speak no evil!"

"Thank heaven for little girls!" "Big boys don't cry!"

"I'm just a girl who can't say no." "Slut!"

"She/he has got to learn sometime."

"Men must be serviced." "Loyalty to family is more important than…"

And the Bible?

"Honor your father and mother."

"Forgive to seventy times seven."

"Spare the rod and spoil the child."

"Take my virgin daughters. Do as you please with them," said Lot to the rapists.

"Turn the other cheek."

"He whom he loveth, he chasteneth."

And the church?

"Forgive and forget."

"Just say a little prayer."

"That's all in the past."

"We don't use words like that in church. It's not nice."

"I forgive you for leading him on."

"Women and children must keep silence in church."

"Christ is the head of the church; man is the head of the woman; woman the head of the children. Those at the bottom of the ladder have no voice."

Or simply: "No comment."

And when the child does speak out?

The mother pretends not to hear, seems deaf and blind. She will often ignore the tell-tale signs like the bitten sweaters and nails, the failing grades, the insomnia, the bedwetting.

The child hears:

"Wash your mouth out with soap and water. Dirty girl!"

"This hurts me more than it hurts you" (said as the strap is applied).

"Keep quiet about it."

"Lock up your mouth!"

"Just give in and bear it!"

"Let sleeping dogs lie."

"Stop sniveling! I'll give you something to cry about."

Archbishop Fulton Sheen said, "Every child should have an occasional pat on the back, as long as it is applied low enough and hard enough!"

If you hear an angry, chastising voice in the supermarket or at the airport or on a beach, you can be pretty sure that when you turn the corner you will see an adult berating a small child. The things adults say to children they would never dream of saying to another adult. Is child abuse on the increase? I do not know. It is much more in the open. A friend tells me of a neighbor tying his son to a tree and thrashing him with a belt in full view of the whole neighborhood back in the 1940s and none of the adults raised a murmur. I doubt that he could get away with it today. Someone would call the local child abuse hotline. There was no such thing when I was growing up.

It is rare for the child to be believed when he or she comes forward with his or her story of abuse. When I did finally tell my mother, she moved in at once and stopped it, threatening my father with the police if he did it again. Why did she create a situation in which I could not tell when it first happened?

I know the answer to this one, because I have worn this Cleopatra mask myself. When my oldest daughter was thirteen years old, and I was enmeshed in the beginnings of my own healing journey but still feeling very much the "victim" (around the "eft" stage), our whole family visited my parents in England. While my husband and I were asleep in another room, my daughter stayed up to watch television with her grandfather, and he tried to rape her. This brave little girl fought him off and told him to f— off! (I did not know such words when I was a little girl. Besides, I was half her age). She then walked about five miles to my cousin Mary's house on the other side of town and made up some extraordinary excuse about why she had arrived on their doorstep in the middle of the night. (She has always been a child of great imagination, concocting the most elaborate lies to cover up the truth—an art form she must have learned from her mother! Says Oscar Wilde, "The truth is rarely pure and never simple!") When she returned home to America, she confided it all to a neighbor, a surrogate mother, who remains to this day the one who understands her in many ways better than I. At school that fall she shared the story with many of her friends, and similar stories of uncles, stepfathers, and big brothers all were hashed over in the lunchroom or when these teenagers were "hanging out"— a healthy way to deal with it.

The only person she did not tell was me, her mother. I found out nearly three years later when I was driving her home from baby-sitting and discussing a paper she was writing for school on rape. Something made me uneasy, and I asked her why she had chosen this subject. Finally she blurted out, "Because it's happened to me!" I stopped the car and cried out for her to tell me who had done this—when—where? "I can't," she said, "because of who it is!" The most awful feeling came across me. I felt myself paralyzed by fear, by ghosts. I could hardly breathe. "It's your father!" she finally blurted out. "He did it to me too!" I said, and we wept together.

Like Harriet, the nineteenth century slave, out of kindness and charity, my daughter had tried to protect me when I had failed to protect her. I believe such courage must make for spiritual maturity, even while it teaches us patterns of deception that are tenacious and terrible. Secrecy is second nature for survivors, for all of us, in one way or another, promised "never to tell." Even sharing with you, the zambuk, is usually done with ancient demon voices ringing in our ears:

"This is just between you and me. You are my special girl and no one needs to know but us two."

"If you tell Mommy she just won't understand, and it might make her even more sick, so you don't tell anyone. This is our secret."

"If you dare say one word about this, I'm going straight to the principal!"

"I'll beat you up if you ever mention this to anyone. Promise me or else…"

But what of the scenario twenty to thirty to forty years later? Perhaps you are still reeling from the news of the abuse, and now the shock has worn off, and even as you acknowledge the courage of the victim, you may still be left with a lingering sense of deception. You too have been caught in the web of lies and cover-ups, secrets and denial just as surely as everyone else in this whole sordid story. You may feel like Pilate: "What is truth?" and have a strong desire to wash your hands of it all, but you can't. This is your spouse or your sister or your friend or your directee of several years or your parishioner. "Why didn't you tell me before?" is a legitimate question, but the answer is always the same: "I told you when I was able."

Now that you have this nasty news dumped in your lap (is that the way it feels?), what to do with it? There may be a strong desire to immediately pass it all on to someone else lock, stock, and barrel, especially a professional. However, the therapist only sees the survivor at set hours, and you probably have to deal with the late night terrors and the early morning flashbacks yourself. Some survivors are very protective of their secret and feel strongly that, though they may have entrusted it to you, it must go no further. I have had several such pro-survivors come to my show and tell me they are there on behalf of someone else who does not even know they are attending. "So you are here for yourself?" I ask, and indeed they are.

The cruel bear stage is a time when you could begin a little research on the subject matter and begin to explore some of your own feelings regarding all this—if you are able. What is also likely to happen is that this story has jolted a fragment of childhood abuse from the deep recesses of your own subconscious, so while you are trying to deal with the survivor's story, you may be caught in a double bind, coping with your own flashbacks. If you are able to share any of this with the survivor, it may be the most healing for both of you. This double-headed dragon can then be faced by the two of you together in different ways (as suggested in the beginning of the last chapter). This happened with my dear friend and fellow actress, Peri Aston. When I was working on my show on abuse, it triggered the following and resulted in her own show on the subject called "Triple Image."

The following is an excerpt from a letter Peri wrote to me:

> I can only say that I refer to it as "my black hole." I am absolutely knocked sideways by the thought that I who always believed I had this perfect childhood may also be an abused child.

That may seem like jumping on the bandwagon, but the more I think of it, the more it resonates in me. I realize I always felt safe, even over-protected within my own family, so perhaps it happened outside the family when I was very young. I find that I can intellectually accept the horror of it, but I have been unable to be in contact with any real feeling about it. You remember your abuse, and it has affected the whole of your life consciously and unconsciously. I just have an intuition. I am trying to remember, tie things up, and let them go. Yours is a reworking. Mine is a searching. My "black hole" is a very tight little ball that I always feel inside of me right in the solar plexus that stops my fully participating in anything and chokes me up whenever I think of it.

Are the cruel bear's paws around the throat so that we can never breathe freely? Did Mary and Joseph sense the ancestral dread as they mounted the temple steps with the child Jesus in their arms? St. Matthew's Gospel begins, "The book of the genealogy of Jesus Christ, the son of David..." What is left unsaid: "...the son of David (king, psalmist, great leader, abuser)."

Yet these good parents stay within the traditions and laws of their people that state: "Every firstborn male shall be deemed to belong to the Lord." Feminists will argue that this discriminates against firstborn female babies and thus invites abuse of little girls, but we have to accept that Mary and Joseph were children of their own time and culture and to have disregarded this law would have meant throwing out the baby with the bath water, quite literally! And when we do follow doggedly within the laws, God surprises us with a Simeon and an Anna.

After Simeon's prophecy, he hands back the child Jesus to his parents and leaves. How devastated, how confused, how mystified Mary and Joseph must have felt! A surprise diversion comes in the form of Anna, age eighty-four, daughter of Phanuel of the Tribe of Asher (a person indeed!), one who has known loss herself as a widow of many years. "She never left the temple, but spent all her time there fasting and praying." When she comes upon the holy family, Luke tells us that immediately light, hope and wisdom spring from Simeon's prophecy for "she talked about him to all who were looking for the restoration of Jerusalem!" This is indeed the Good News—no sad, sick secret, but the coming of the Holy Spirit that will usher in the new age.

Is there an "Anna" in your life? Time and time again after I have performed my show on Julian of Norwich (another medieval Anna), people have come to me saying, "I came here tonight feeling so burdened, and this message was just what I needed." Pilate did have a choice. He could have delayed the execution, talked it over with his wife, summoned holy men and women for their opinions. So do we. If we are truly protective of ourselves, as well as those we love, then we can let the awful secret sit for a while and do nothing except be very open and receptive to the mystery of suffering. Maybe we need to hibernate for a while, take time off from listening to anyone, and, like the bear, avert our eyes. The cruelty of child abuse, when we ponder it deeply in our hearts, is a terrible mystery, part of our human condition, I believe.

Even young children can be extraordinarily cruel to one another, especially in a mob when the excitement grows out of control, and we are part of that society too. I have had to avert my eyes on many occasions from television specials, newspaper articles that well-meaning friends have sent on "the subject," books thrust into my hands that I *must* read. Yes, it is a cruel world out there, but then I remind myself that most parents do not abuse their children, and for every awful family secret there are many more "triumphs." Of course, these do not reach the headlines, but occasionally we catch a glimpse of Jerusalem even in the most unlikely places. This may encourage you to relate charitably towards the enabler, be it Mother Church, Mother herself, or whoever was responsible for the child and failed to provide the protection. I have often heard people proclaim in righteous indignation, "The one I'd like to talk to is the mother! Couldn't she see what was going on?" No, she couldn't, weighted down as she is by the huge web of pretense and denial, ponderous and slow as an old bear. When the survivor does begin to see the role of the enabler, he or she is much too dependent, too fragile to think of confronting him or her just now, but that time will come.

Avoidance may be the only way you can deal with a cruel bear, and particularly if you are a man, whether victim, abuser, or pro-survivor. Avoidance contains the word "void." This may be a transitional space allowing you to distance and protect yourself until the time to deal with the pain is ripe—and men are very apt in this strategy. They distance themselves from the too-painful reality by pretending not to hear. In the church, men in leadership positions can hide from messy, bloody issues such as child abuse behind brocaded gowns, miters, Canon Law, Bible quotes, secretaries, cloisters, and locked doors. Perhaps it is also biological, because men do not have to face the pain of childbirth. This is one of the reasons women stayed at the foot of the cross, while a big man like Peter, who in one instance could leap into the water to meet his Master, could not bring himself to climb Calvary and be there when Jesus was dying.

How many "Peters" today are sniveling in some upper room, nursing their pain, when if only they could get up and focus on another's greater sorrow, they could move themselves up and beyond? It is well known that men are more reluctant to seek counseling than are women, and if you are a woman trying to be present to a male survivor, you may well receive the cold shoulder. With a celibate man, he will often invite an intimacy that is then denied or avoided. He does not call when he says he will, procrastinates, feigns being too busy, retreats into an all-male environment, and shuts the door on you very firmly. Yet this is the same man who broke down and cried in your arms two weeks ago! The body language will often speak volumes. Allergies will suddenly appear, or shingles, nervous overeating, drinking, smoking. He can't find his glasses, his homily, his address book. And that habit he developed as a little boy of rocking back and forth on his heels or pounding his thigh while he's trying to make a point seems more pronounced. You see it all. What can you do?

As did the serving maid who confronts Peter in the courtyard during Jesus's trial and immediately sees through his cock-and-bull story (interesting male metaphor!) about "not knowing the man," keep on asking the hard questions. (Did she perhaps overhear the weeping and become suspicious?) Someone said to Peter early Easter morning, "Get off your duff, go down to the tomb, and stop feeling sorry for yourself!" (In my imagination that was Mary, the mother of Jesus.)

If men avoid the pain, we women have mistressed the art of embracing the hurt, picking at the wound, and examining it all from every angle. We are often masochistic, rehearsing a scene over and over again, relishing every detail, nursing our dirty little secrets like nasty pets, or we may enjoy our suffering in silence, martyr-like. A poem by a survivor speaks of this "hard unsanctified distress":

> Her lips were open—not a sound
> Came through the parted lines of red.
> Whate'er it was, the hideous wound
> In silence and in secret bled.
> No sigh relieved her speechless woe;
> She had no voice to speak her dread.
> —Mary Elizabeth Coleridge

I believe this masochism is very off-putting for men. They hate it, and it leads to avoidance very quickly. How many wives can attest to their husband's seeming cruelty when they are weeping copiously, and the tears only make him angry or worse still, indifferent: It is a romantic and unhealthy zambuk who rushes to join in the masochistic rituals of many survivors at this stage. Hand them a Kleenex with no comment or cut through the crap (if you will pardon my profanity) as Jesus did when the women called out, "Blessed is the womb that bore you and the breasts that gave you suck!" "No, rather blessed is she who hears the word of God and does it!" he replied.

What is the "word of God" to the enabler, the victim, the pro-survivor? It will be as ranging as in every circumstance, but one thing is sure. If we are to continue in this journey together, we all have to move onto the next stage of the journey: the mighty lion.

The collect for the third Sunday in Advent in the Episcopal Church (commonly called "stir up Sunday") begins: "Stir up your power, O Lord, and with great might come among us." We must now confront the central issue in all child abuse—power. The soul, at this stage, is on the threshold of the "terrible twos," that time when psychologists tell us that the greater part of our development is taking place. It was around this time in my own healing journey that I found solace in Jesus's parable of the widow and the unjust judge (Luke 18:1-8). "And he told them a parable to the effect that they ought always to pray and not lose heart." I give you my version of the story, written to address the avoidance (as I saw it) of my friend and spiritual director at the time:

> She had tried to explain it to him hundreds of times. The problem was, of course, words. He simply didn't listen—but shut out the sound of her voice and went on his own sweet way.
>
> So what to do when you're right at the bottom of the ladder, female, a widow, with no man to support you in a world run by men? Big men dressed up in impressive costumes with awesome titles: Your Honor, Your Grace, Your Excellency?
>
> And just getting to them—the endless lines, the secretaries that protected the bishops' offices, the judges' chambers. All the most important men seemed to be inaccessible and overprotected—but most of all, uncaring.
>
> He just didn't give a damn!
>
> But, she thought, my cause is just. I have to

reach him somehow. So she tossed and turned all night, pondering it deeply in her heart. "Maybe your cause isn't just after all," said Demon Number One.

"Maybe you should just give up and stay home and be a good girl," said Demon Number Two.

Said Demon Number Three (she always turned up around three in the morning, and her fantasy knew no bounds): "How about the judge's head on a platter with french fries and a nice fat pickle?"

Came the light of dawn, as the sun rose over Mount Zion, a still small voice inside her (she called her Gabriel) said, "Don't be afraid, Roberta. Don't give up now. Judgment belongs to God alone, and with God all things are possible. Now, sweetie, this calls for action, so listen carefully."

And the angel whispered a long, long whisper in her ear. And the widow began to smile, and titter, and giggle like a little girl, because the plan was so simple and yet so, well, miraculous.

"How can this be happening to me?" she thought to herself. So when she finally made her way to see the Big Man himself (of course he wasn't looking), she remembered that angel voice: "This calls for action."

And act she did, with tears and sobbing and falling on the ground and practically fainting and begging and pleading with her hands outstretched and hair tumbling in her eyes. She had even considered rending her garments—but when you're poor, you just can't afford to go that far. Oh, it was amazing to see! Salome herself could not have done better!

> *Thought the Great Man: "This woman is so great a nuisance, she has quite worn me out with her persistence! I shall have to see her righted."*
> *And he finally began to listen.*
> *As she said to her sister the next day: "You see. Prayer changes things!"*

You will notice that my solution to the problem was a two-year-old's temper tantrum. Is there a patron saint for two-year-olds who can help us all through this trying time? As infinite patience is needed, you might turn to one of the great women who founded religious orders, such as Catherine McCauley, founder of the Sisters of Mercy, or Marguerite, founder of the Grey Nuns. But, to my mind, the mother of Methodism, Susannah Wesley—a frail eighteenth century English woman who bore nineteen children (including the great Charles and John Wesley) and taught them all a "method" that was the foundation of that denomination—shows the truly caring and nurturing spirit that we all need in these difficult days. Susannah regularly set aside two hours a day for quiet and solitary prayer but said that, "Religion is not to be confined to church or closet, but everywhere I am in thy presence, Lord."

Such firmness and wisdom can give us faith sufficient to grapple with mighty lions! Susannah Wesley, pray for us! For what we need now is a "method," or, if you will, an "order" that will keep us all in grace. As Dietrich Bonhoeffer said, it is marriage, the institution, that keeps love alive, especially in difficult days, and not the other way around.

hold me fast

don't let me pass

IV THE MIGHTY LION:

A POWER STRUGGLE

ake a look at the painting (see next page) that I did at the age of thirteen. It is "Christmas Shopping," winter of 1954. The black lines that are so prevalent were a last-minute inspiration. I remember the feeling of satisfaction I had when I painted them in and thus defined the chaotic crowd scene. Later in my teens, while I was a student at theater school, I was undergoing great traumas at home. My mother gave birth to my severely spastic sister, Jessica, and had her first serious attempt at suicide. When I was nineteen, I stayed up all night painting the scenery for a student production of a living room comedy. At dawn, exhausted and frustrated by the boring red roses on the wallpaper pattern, I suddenly picked up a pot of black paint and put dark lines around all my roses in the style of the symbolic

Painting done by the author when she was in class Upper IIIa, Turbridge Wells Grammar School for Girls.

French painter Georges Rouault or the medieval artists of stained glass where the lead lines define the colors and shapes. I shall never forget the joy I felt when I stepped back and saw that the black lines had brought depth and life and interest to this boring set. To hear Jonny Lee, the Scots scenic design teacher, praise "Roberta [with rolled R's] and her bonny red roses that pick up the light, ye, ken!" mirrored my own satisfaction that out of the ordinary, dreary, everyday living room chaos came order, form, and—yes—darkness bringing forth light. Advent into Christmas and onto Epiphany!

This thirteen-year-old's painting helped me to remember the precise time that I had told my mother about the abuse: September 1954. Three months later, I painted this picture. "To everything there is a season," and so I understand now that the seeds for that creative response had been sown in much earlier times, perhaps even at the age of three. I have vivid memories of World War II: of running through the garden at night in a little blue robe with a rabbit sewn on the pocket, holding my mother's

A V-Day party on the author's street, London Road, Southborough, Kent.

hand to reach the air-raid shelter as the bombs were falling; of hiding under the kitchen table with my grandmother, wearing our gas masks; of the mean woman who spanked my bottom for using her clothesline for play when my mother and I were evacuated to her house in the country because the south of London was too dangerous....

Yet it was not all chaos. I have a yellowed newspaper clipping from 1944 that reports on the nursery school I attended: "The head mistress was presented with a bunch of roses by Roberta Dolby, youngest pupil." We learned French! Would you believe that while the bombs fell, nice English ladies taught three-year-olds to sing "Frère Jacques" and chant "Je suis une fille; vous êtes un garçon"?

To this day, I speak French well and with a good accent (at least for an English woman!). The discipline and order of school has always stood me in good stead. I like writing this book for Abbey Press, where up the hill from the printing presses and publications offices the monks of the archabbey chant and pray the offices in the ordered routine of the Benedictine way of life. Writing this book I seem to have lived again through the experiences of which I tell. This chapter is being written while recovering from the gynecological surgery I mentioned in the previous chapter, so I have been rendered powerless by the mighty lion of modern hospitals and all the insurance business, anesthetics, nursing, painkillers, and after-care that are part of that scene. Unlike the little girl who submitted silently to the doctor and his shiny instruments, the woman has *chosen* this way. I'm putting black lines around my roses and standing firm before the mighty lion.

Whether survivor or zambuk, you need some kind of system, order, or method to sustain you in this dangerous stage of the mighty lion, a grounding that will allow you and your Janet to grapple with this king of beasts, feet firmly planted, strong arms to engage, and eyes that look steadfastly beyond to the new life— the "baby." The most enduring spiritualities have been based on a reordering of our priorities, understanding where the true power is hidden. All of monasticism is based on this, stemming from St. Benedict and his rule and flowering into all the diverse religious orders. Think of the Jesuits, where the spiritual exercises of St. Ignatius have shaped and reordered the inner man (or woman). Protestants too have had their "Method"-ists, their Quakers (based on a "quaking," a waiting in the orderliness of silence upon the Holy Spirit), and my own Anglicans—all of our life and worship is based on "The Book of Common Prayer," a little book of monastic prayers so well-thumbed and beloved in most Episcopal churches. The mendicant orders like the Salvation Army are organized down to roll call, uniforms, and marching bands. The twelve-step programs require persons to admit that they are powerless and that only a Higher Power can bring order from the chaos. A spirituality that faithfully addresses abusive power will succeed.

In the twentieth century, psychology's "methods" have found increasing popularity within the churches. There is scarcely a serious Christian anywhere today who does not have some inkling of their standing with Myers-Briggs, the Jungian "method," or the Enneagram. This latter system, derived from the Sufis and appropriated by Jesuits, Dominicans, and many others, has proven extremely helpful for many of us, especially in the middle of our lives, when, Dante tells us, we enter that "dark wood." His *Divine Comedy* with its three-tiered system (heaven, purgatory, and hell) has enlightened millions over the centuries. Other great writers like Teresa of Avila, Thomas Merton, Evelyn Underhill, and William Shakespeare all derived much of their creative power from the order of their lives.

Yes, I include Shakespeare because theater and acting are based very firmly on discipline. In the middle of a performance of the play *All That I Am*, on the lives of such unsung heroines of the church as St. Peter's wife and St. Augustine's mistress, I was suddenly interrupted by a fanatical voice crying out, "She's from the devil! It's all lies! Don't listen to that evil woman!" The large Roman Catholic church was packed with people, and for a long moment I lost all control and wanted to burst into tears and rush offstage. But the voice of the principal of my theater school of thirty years ago reminded me in clipped British tones: "You are a professional! This is an art form! The show must go on, and you have a responsibility to your audience." I felt all eyes turn back to me as the woman was evicted, and suddenly the forgotten lines returned to my head and I felt a great surge of strength and made it through to the end of the play and a standing ovation. It was as if the fanatical woman had thrown a knife at me which struck the groin and left me bleeding in public, in the middle of my beautiful play, and it left me feeling like a hurt child, until I remembered who I really am. After it all, I collapsed in the sacristy and sobbed out—to a warm motherly woman, a zambuk—the whole story of my sexual abuse and how this felt just the same. "My dear," she said, "I was ordained a priest just yesterday, and this is sacrifice; this is what it is all about."

Many adult survivors seem to act like two-year-olds around this part of the healing, and that is an age when we all learned control over this extraordinary world of big chairs that must be climbed into, stairs that must be assayed one at a time while you hold on carefully, sand that can be made into castles or thrown in your sister's eyes, water around which you may so easily lose balance and drown, and above all, those two-legged adults that must be looked up to. The average two- or three-year-old reaches to the top of my thighs—that is their world view. It is also a time of extreme frustration when almost anything can trigger a temper tantrum. Adults seem to be in control of everything—the leading reins pulling the child this way and that.

If you, the zambuk, are in the midst of a big power struggle within your own life at this stage, then probably the kindest thing you can do for your survivor is to say, "no," and like a frazzled parent, provide the child with a good day care facility or trained nurse. When both of you are feeling weak and powerless, your pain will clash with your survivor's pain, and the resulting transference and counter-transference will leave you both devastated. This happened to me when I went to lead a retreat for survivors. I was promised a priest co-leader, but he made it only for the Mass. We had a terrible blizzard, and I felt like a mother with too many children locked into that retreat house. The "older ones" did well, but one or two very fragile people became angry that I was not attending to their needs as they had anticipated. One woman, instead of confronting me there and then, returned home to her therapist, who wrote me a letter admonishing me for not caring for his client: "You need help yourself, lady!" he said. It was true. I did.

The comparison between a full-size lion and a baby deer is an appropriate one. The one on the side watching the struggle might feel that the little deer has no chance of escape, and this is true.

When we were little and powerless, a greater terrifying force overpowered us. Unlike the deer in the paws of the lion, this is *not* part of nature's plan. An alien and unnatural violence is passed from generation to generation, like the chain of abuse that I use in *Masks and Mirrors*, made up of many different hands, all joined together by the plastic (nonbiodegradable) rings that hold together the six-packs of beer. The unconscious drunken state that all these beer cans represent is also what holds together the chain. How can the chains be broken? The patterns of learned helplessness, giving away one's power that was established in childhood—how can they be changed?

Who is the mighty lion?

King of all the beasts, beloved in the Western world (where we seldom see it except in captivity) as a symbol, a coat of arms. The "scion" in the poem, Janet's inheritance, is in fact her place in the ancient and noble family to which she belongs: her ancestors and ancestresses. The lion—magnificent, single-minded, and ruthless in the wild; desolate, defeated, and tragic in captivity. Incest and rape are essentially power issues. When Tam Lin becomes the mighty lion, Janet must hold fast to this enormous, potentially dangerous animal. The adult survivor, likewise, when faced with the "Ultimate Power Struggle," whatever that may be for him or her—confronting the perpetrator, the power struggles within family, church, work—must hold fast to the idea that this is a matter of life and death: "I am your baby's father." She or he must be as protective of her or his new self as a lioness with an unborn cub. A prayer might be like Louis MacNeice's poem:

> PRAYER BEFORE BIRTH
> I am not yet born; O hear me.
> Let not the bloodsucking bat or the rat
> or the stoat or the club-footed ghoul
> come near me.
>
> I am not yet born, console me.
> I fear that human race may with tall
> walls wall me.
> With strong drugs dope me, with wise
> lies lure me
> on black racks rack me, in blood-baths
> roll me.

I am not yet born; provide me
With water to dandle me, grass to grow
for me, trees to talk
to me, sky to sing to me, birds and a
white light
in the back of my mind to guide me.

I am not yet born; forgive me
For the sins that in me the world shall
commit, my words
when they speak me, my thoughts when
they think me,
my treason engendered by traitors
beyond me,
my life when they murder by
means of my
hands, my death when they live me.

I am not yet born; rehearse me
In the parts I must play and the cues I
must take when
old men lecture me, bureaucrats hector
me, mountains
frown at me, lovers laugh at me, the
white
waves call me to folly and the
desert calls
me to doom and the beggar refuses
my gift and my children curse
me.

I am not yet born; O hear me,
Let not the man who is beast or who
thinks he is God come near me.

I am not yet born; O fill me

With strength against those who would
freeze my
humanity, would dragoon me into a
lethal automaton,
would make me a cog in a machine,
a thing with
one face, a thing, and against all
those
who would dissipate my entirety,
would
blow me like thistledown
hither and
thither or hither and thither
like water held in the
hands would spill me.

Let them not make me a stone and let
them not spill me.
Otherwise kill me.

—Louis MacNeice
(Springboard, 1944)

The abused child is used by the adult as an object. The abused child is "stone" or spilled "like water held in the hands." In Matthew's Gospel, we read of the Holy Innocents used as dispensable objects to protect the power of the mighty lion: Herod.

Holy Innocents—not a feast day known for packed churches and fervent prayers among the faithful! Why is it not considered important? Why will a lecture on abortion by a famous person draw a standing-room-only crowd at church while a talk on child sexual abuse will raise only a handful, if that? If you asked most church leaders, I believe they would tell you that they are concerned about child abuse, but most are so heavily into denial, they cannot see the truth. Likewise, many partners, like my mother, would have considered themselves caring, concerned people. The parallel with drunken driving is pertinent. It is only *after* the car crash and the innocent victim is pulled dead from the other car that the drunken driver and his or her family finally acknowledge the problem. It may take a heroic story of child sexual abuse to be publicly acclaimed by some important and well-known church leader before the church sits up and takes notice. What if the Archbishop of Canterbury preached a sermon this Holy Innocents Day telling a story of the child abuse that he suffered? Or Mother Teresa, in her old age (when such memories do return), told of sexual abuse by a family member when she was young? Or Billy Graham? One of the best little books on the subject was written by none other than Jimmy Swaggart, and maybe, if the book is from personal experience, it sheds light on some of his sexual misdemeanors in later life. In Rahway Prison, the child molesters who persist longest in denial are the priests and ministers, the religious ones, the psychologist tells me. Jesus is constantly trying to break through to the truth with the Scribes and Pharisees, "those whited sepulchers." He said, "Beware of the leaven of the Pharisees, which is hypocrisy. Nothing is covered up that will not be revealed or hidden that will not be known. Whatever you have said in the dark shall be heard in the light, and what you have whispered in private rooms shall be proclaimed upon the housetops." We have that promise from Jesus that God's truth in this matter will some day break through all our denial. Every family, every individual has "secret sins," many of which we cannot even bring ourselves to recognize, and when this happens, the Herods of this world will no longer use their power to destroy families through child abuse.

What were the feelings of Mary and Joseph, the survivors of the Holy Innocents tragedy? Their child had been protected through angels and dreams, but did he himself cause these innocent deaths? This is a difficult story in contemplating the meaning of pain from a Christian standpoint. Was Rachel's weeping for her children part of the Divine Plan within the mind of God? The paralyzing guilt of many pro-survivors when hearing of innocent suffering is mirrored by the survivors themselves. I have a terrible time dealing with stories and pictures of the Holocaust.

I was so traumatized when I visited Maidenek, a concentration camp in Poland, that afterwards I had nightmares and contemplated suicide.

I was twenty-three, and I still remember vividly the huge mound of children's shoes—all 1940s style—that were the sole remains of these Holy Innocents. "How can I continue to live in a world like this?" I thought. In speaking with other adult survivors of childhood abuse, I find many of them recoil in terror at pictures of Auschwitz. During the last war in the Persian Gulf, I was plunged into deep depression, especially during the bombing raids. Hearing that women and children were in the shelter that was bombed by the allies left me with a sense of powerlessness and despair that I knew connected with my childhood. Here I was in a situation in which my government was acting as an abuser, not only against people in Iraq and Kuwait, but against our own citizens. By focusing on an outside "enemy," our government was able to distract attention and divert resources from some of our own most vital needs, such as health care, housing, and education. The (mostly young) people in the military were exposed to violence and forced to do violence, the effects of which they will have to live with all their lives.

Public response to this government-initiated abuse is similar to that of survivors of sexual abuse: numbness, avoidance, inability to pay attention to the grim reality; many of us opposed to the war feeling terribly isolated, strangers in our own land.

From the onset of the war, I found that the news reports and the speeches of the military spokespersons and government officials mirrored my experience of abuse so closely that my deep, habitual responses to abuse were triggered. I went numb. I wanted to escape the reality of the war through inattentiveness. I became anxious and depressed. I was gripped with the old chronic fear of humiliation and of being dismissed, which made it all but impossible to write letters to my senators, my representative, or the president.

Other survivors of abuse may find themselves locked in the grip of their habitual obedience to people in positions of authori-

ty. They may find themselves in a panic about expressing dis-
agreement with prevailing opinion about the war. They may anes-
thetize their discomfort with alcohol, food, or compulsive behaviors. They may go into denial, either minimizing the effect of the
war or reframing the war as a necessary and just action, rather
than a gross and overt form of abuse. Many of us fall into the
automatic patterns of silence that protected us as children (but
mainly protect the abusers now). Almost all of us will have to
struggle with our distorted ability to recognize abuse and our lack
of clarity about what is healthy.

I performed my show *Masks and Mirrors* during the war in
the Persian Gulf and developed terrible abscesses, herpes in the
mouth, and a persistent insomnia that sent me to a kind of 3 a.m.
hell where I raged inwardly at President Bush, General
Schwarzkopf, and Saddam Hussein. Mostly, however, I believe it
was not only the sense of responsibility and helplessness (if only
I had been "better," prayed "harder," it could have been prevented!) but above all the dreadful power of Evil (war) over the little
ones of this world. The chaos that ensues in the aftermath of any
war is the outward and visible sign of an inner chaos that we survivors know only too well. If rape is a sister to war, then incest
and child abuse are daughters and sons. My father returned home
not only from fighting in World Wars I and II but from thirty
years of soldiering as a sergeant major. One of the spoils of war
is rape. You win the battle, you go in and rape the women and
children. There are several stories of this in the Hebrew
Scriptures. In that exultant power, the triumphant phallus does
not discriminate: it must be satisfied. How do you then go home
to your wife in a nice feather bed and to the dailiness of life, perhaps with no employment and no military orders? A tremendous
feeling of let-down and frustration must ensue. Where is the
glamour? Illicit and exciting sex is like war, and the secrecy is not
only for protection, but for the thrill of it. This too makes the
abuser feel powerful, even as it weakens the victim and fills the
victim with dread.

How can we find some ordinary time when it feels like Good

Friday? The summer of 1986, I was supposed to have gone away on an eight-day retreat to do the Spiritual Exercises of St. Ignatius. Instead, I contended with the cruel bear all that long, hot summer. On St. Ignatius Day, July 31, I was complaining loud and long to a good friend (and zambuk) of how I *needed* those exercises, and now it was denied me! "You pray to St. Ignatius," he said. "He will answer your prayer." I was somewhat cynical about this and muttered to him that we Anglicans can go to the Direct Source, thank you very much. However, "the system" works beautifully whether or not we fully assent to it, and by September, when I was up and about, I had met the perfect spiritual director for me at that time, and I had begun the Nineteenth Annotation—the exercises in thirty weeks instead of thirty days. In writing this book, I have again needed "a system." Sister Agnes Mallner, O.S.U., died two years ago, and I feel her presence with me now as I renew the exercises with a different spiritual director. Instead of my keeping a journal as was required by the first exercises, Sister Gerri is asking me to paint and write about my prayer life—and with my left (non-dominant) hand.

One of the physical manifestations of childhood sexual abuse is imbalance. I have found this to be true for many survivors. I am overly right-handed; I cannot hear properly from my left ear; I have a tendency to smile crookedly, and it's almost impossible for me to be grounded. I always stand on one foot, especially when I am waiting for someone. All this I learned as a little girl. Watch the body language of children on line, and, if you are observant, you can tell who comes from a dysfunctional family.

God, the ground of our being, is suddenly distanced from us when the abuse takes place. It is almost as if the mighty lion knocks us over the first time the abuse occurs, and we have to pull ourselves together and pick ourselves off the ground. This leaves us feeling very shaky, to put it mildly but succinctly. "Shaky" is a very good word to describe many survivors at this stage. Like the toddler, we have only just learned to walk, and if we try to run, we will fall flat on our faces.

What can the zambuk do when confronted by "temper

tantrums"? Often your survivor will appear to be out of control at this stage in the healing journey. This will manifest itself in such ways as screaming at children, spouse, and especially you, the zambuk. Just as the two-year-old does not understand and cannot fully communicate why he or she is feeling so bad, neither can the adult survivor trying to gain control of the situation. I just returned from the South Bronx today, where many people feel trapped and powerless. I saw many more frayed tempers, heard much more cursing and abusive language than I ever hear in my suburban area. Everything is out in the open in the Bronx.

I believe the ultimate power struggle we all face is also the one that Jesus faced in the desert, and he could not—did not—truly begin his ministry until he had been through that time. Ringing in his ears were the words that came through the Holy Spirit at Baptism: "You are my beloved son." For all those hidden years, from the time of twelve when he began to grasp his relationship to a Father beyond his earthly father, Joseph, Jesus waited for this moment. The relationship is now so close that God becomes "Abba" for Jesus from now on, but this does not come about easily. At this stage in our struggle, if there is a glimmer of hope, we then can also accept the adoption by "Abba—the Father" who will sustain us through the difficult days ahead.

Driven by the Holy Spirit into the desert to confront his mighty lion, Jesus remembers three ultimate temptations. There may have been others, but, if so, either these are the ones he chose to share or else these are the ones that the Gospel writers deemed worthy of report. The first temptation, "Tell these stones to become bread," from the viewpoint of a victim of childhood abuse is about the emptiness, hunger, and loss that we experience during this stage. To paraphrase from the lyrics of the Rolling Stones: "We can't get no satisfaction." Like the prodigal son, we have "wasted ourselves in reckless living," and it may take a foreign landowner and his unorthodox pigs to bring us to our senses. I always feel the youngest son began his journey home to his father when he stood on the unemployment line for that menial, despised work as the pig man and accepted the job.

The landowner acted as zambuk to the prodigal son, forcing him to eat the pig husks and confront all that this nicely brought up Jewish boy must have found loathsome. He had to do this through his senses, just as Jesus had to experience that terrible hunger for stones to become bread. "And no one gave him anything." You, the zambuk, may have to watch your survivor doing terrible things physically, sensationally, before they can emerge from their desert. Here are some of the possibilities:

• Severe eating disorders like anorexia or bulimia that finally come to the place where hospitalization is necessary. Will you drive them there? Pay a visit?

• Obesity is often a sign of childhood abuse. Many adult survivors have been "eating stones" as a way of oral gratification for years. Around this mighty lion stage, your overweight friend suffers a heart attack or is refused a job because he or she cannot manage it physically or suffers some humiliation at the hands of someone they care about. Will you put them in touch with some kind of system or order that will address this fat issue?

• Amazing stress and overwork. Your survivor will be over burdened to such an extent that a good old-fashioned nervous breakdown is perhaps the only way out.

• Smoking, alcoholism, and drug abuse are all related to this first temptation, and today there are many support systems in place to help this disorder. The mighty lion stage is an appropriate time to go to Smoke Enders or A.A. or drug abuse counseling, all of which invoke the help of a Higher Power.

At a recent retreat were a zambuk (a social worker) and a celebrant (a woman with two little children). Two years previously, this young mother had arrived drunk and disorderly (again!) with her two babies at the doors of the homeless shelter. In spite of knowing the "no alcohol" rules of the shelter, she managed to slip out and bring in a bottle. Near midnight, the social worker finally turned her out into the streets in the middle of winter with her two babies.

She wandered about all night until at dawn, she fell on her knees, bleeding and weak, and began to face reality. The social worker said it was the best and most difficult thing she had ever done in her whole life. Could you have made that choice? All of Jesus's responses to the devil in the three temptations in the desert involve a "no" or "Thou shalt not," and all of us are included in this. Perhaps a sister or brother came to Jesus in the desert, bearing a delicious piece of challah, smothered in butter and honey and he had to say "no."

• The most common bodily disorders are quite naturally of a sexual nature. The flashbacks of the eft stage now become manifested in manifold troubles in adult life. It may take a hospital visit to close up a sinus duct in the vulva that was created through childhood abuse forty years earlier, as in my case. Or the gay man may be picked up by the police for cruising or finally confront that huge stack of pornographic magazines stashed under the bed. Or the married woman may at last be able to explain to her husband why she fears to be pregnant or blanks out entirely during intercourse. Or the monk may preach a hysterical anti-abortion homily that we realize has more to do with *his* issues of childhood abuse.

There are as many sexual disorders as there are victims and I am not a sex therapist—nor are you, I presume. Your survivor may need some professional help in this area and this will be the time to make that phone call if it has not been made already. Neither of you will find any satisfaction unless you do something, and the time for taking a nice long walk or baking a batch of cookies is long past. Know that just as the father in the parable of the prodigal son was home waiting and praying during all those terrible hours in the pig pen or that the Holy Spirit was hovering over Jesus when he lay in the desert, weak and famished, toying with those stones, so is God tenderly watching over all of us at this time, "holding fast."

Just when we feel that we are lowest of the low, the mighty lion appears in another guise. This time it seems as if we are surrounded by huge, hostile crowds like the ones that drove Jesus up to the pinnacle of the temple. This is a most precarious place, and again how little and powerless we are! The devil uses our own words: "Scripture says" to persuade us that the easy, fairy-tale publicity stunt—jumping off the temple pinnacle into the incredulous crowds below—will make it all better. Note, too, that this "desert" temptation takes place in the midst of the teeming life of the city, not a retreat in some secluded place. What the devil promises as a cushion against the pain—"They will bear you in their arms lest you dash your foot against a stone"—in actual fact comes to Jesus *after* he has emerged from the desert when, we are told, "the angels came and ministered to him."

Jesus is in pain and weak from his loss when he peers over the edge of the pinnacle and contemplates this—could it be suicide? He has not yet performed any of the miracles that prove his powers to himself as well as others, so how would this "I'll show them who I am" stunt bring about all the easy, fake messiahship the devil suggests? With no cross at the end of the road?

I cannot write a book about adult survival without mentioning the extreme ways that we contemplate to gain attention and numb the pain and fear. I have already spoken of times when suicide has been in my thoughts, though never as dire as many survivors I know. What ultimately persuaded Jesus to turn his back on the city below and descend the steps of the temple and enter the mainstream of Jerusalem life? His reply, "You shall not tempt the Lord your God," is very direct and simple. He says "no" and accepts the responsibility of all that is to follow in the next three years. This is a lonely decision but one that only he can make; we do not hear that he brought anyone else with him. Certainly there would have been no Transfiguration without this pinnacle experience first, and that pinnacle experience he shared with three others.

I don't believe anyone can really prevent a very tormented, suicidal person from actually commiting suicide, but I think we can create a climate in which the "no" seems possible. I must tell you the story of Ann, an intelligent, attractive Irish woman who grew up on a farm in Ireland and was abused by a farmhand as a child. When she was in her early thirties and working as a nanny, hoping for a green card in the U.S., I was one of several people who tried to befriend her. Last summer, I heard that Ann had renounced many of her friends and spiritual ties and came out as a militant lesbian. At last she had found the protection and identity she craved. But an affair with another woman turned sour, and after her lover told her that she cared for someone else, she took a gun and shot herself.

This tragic act—could it have been prevented? I was a distant zambuk, and Ann felt distanced from me because I had insisted that forgiveness was part of the healing when Ann had instigated legal procedures against the farmhand. This brought no satisfaction. She was very vulnerable.

I have some experience with suicide attempts, as my maternal grandmother walked into the sea and drowned herself when I was eleven, and my mother had several dramatic suicide attempts, one of which involved lying down on the railroad tracks as a train full of passengers approached. The driver nearly had an accident, so my father was called to account and yet again my mother ended up in the mental hospital. The only thing that I can think of that might have turned Ann and my mother from their "see me" suicidal dramas was an appeal from someone more helpless and needy than themselves. Both of them were very good with babies, and if the woman in the first temptation story had staggered up to either of them with her two crying infants and thrust them into their arms, I believe they would have accepted the challenge and moved beyond their own tiny suicidal world back into "Jerusalem life" again.

The last time I myself felt suicidal was after viewing the movie on Archbishop Oscar Romero and El Salvador. I said to the nun who accompanied me (she had been in El Salvador), "Is it *all* Good Friday?" "Yes," she said. That night of despair and terror in Buffalo, New York, turned to hope in the morning when "angels came and ministered to me." As I picked up my car at Newark Airport and drove down the New Jersey Turnpike to my next engagement, I distinctly heard a voice in my right ear telling me to let go of El Salvador since there was nothing I could do and start to work on my show for incest survivors since that was something I *could* do. The soldiers who raped and killed innocent people had all been little boys, and who knows what homes they had come from? Since my own government was implicated in the war in El Salvador, to "brighten the corner where you are," as the song says, was the only way out. When I think back to that time, I remember that the seeds for this sprouting of new life were planted at Newark Airport by the porter who helped me with my bags and smiled at me, saying, "Now you take care." He "brightened my corner" and acted as zambuk. Even a smile will work miracles!

The third but not last temptation specifically involved the power issue. We are told "the devil took him up to a high place"—from the victims' view, the perpetrators always seemed above us, large and looming, like a mighty lion—"and showed him in a flash all the kingdoms of the world." Whenever Jesus speaks of "the world," he seems to limit it to those principalities and powers held beneath the devil's sway, not to some lovely universal vision like that of "earth rise," seen by the men who went to the moon, or Julian's world held like a hazelnut in the hand of the Creator, the Lover, the Sustainer. I like the New English Bible translation "in a flash" as it reminds me of the "flashbacks" of adult survivors to those times of childhood abuse and, again and again, when the pattern of powerlessness is repeated in our adulthood. The devil lays before Jesus the invitation to bow down and worship him in exchange for all of this worldly kingdom below. As with the other two temptations, Jesus searches in his memory and replies, "It is written you shall do homage to the Lord your God. God alone shall you worship."

The foundation for this response was made back in his childhood when he was taken to the synagogue and learned the Psalms and stories of his people that were to sustain him, all the way through to "My God, my God, why hast thou forsaken me?" on the cross. If there is no sense of God's power when we are growing up and if we are rendered absolutely powerless (as Alice Miller believes Hitler experienced as a child growing up in a severely dysfunctional family with a father who abused him and a mother so weak she failed to protect him), we have no answer but "yes" to the devil. Our prisons are filled with such people. And wars are fought because little boys like Saddam Hussein were tortured by their stepfathers or because George Bush could never please his powerful, exacting father. When the power is from the devil, the adult survivor may have to respond in drastic measures that require David-like tactics to overthrow our Goliaths.

Jesus and David both came from families where care and wisdom were such that they remembered who they were in times of crisis. Many adult survivors see themselves as totally helpless. They have given away so much power there is none left, or so they think. They may even try to dump it all on you, the zambuk. Keep repeating at this stage, "You give me too much power." Is there a "little stone" to make a catapult that pierces the power of the abuser? What is the nature of this process? One way that I have found most effective in retreats is to ask survivors to think back and remember just one moment of grace and power from their childhood. Now some may protest that there was none; all "the world" was against them. This is another ploy of the "devil." We all have our "Moments of Being" when we were "King of the Castle" and the rest of the world were "dirty rascals." Some of us may have found our power in nature, as many poets and artists have done; or in religious experience, as saints like Teresa of Avila or Agnes have done; or in writing, like Ann Frank or Virginia Woolf; or in music, like Mozart or Mahler; or in science, like Einstein; or, for me, in the power of playacting and theater. The local newspaper said, "The whole stage came to life when the wicked witch arrived!" I was the wicked witch.

The method I have used successfully on retreats, when I feel we are at this stage, is to put people into pairs to tell each other their stories of childhood power and then into fours where two stories are related, one from each couple. The second time the chosen story is told, it is in the third person by the one who previously listened: "Once upon a time there was a little girl called _____." I then ask the quartet to choose the most dramatic story and act it out, using as many props, costumes, music, and sound effects as they can gather together in half an hour. The sharing of these sacred tales is always a time of grace and enlightenment for all concerned.

With my background of teaching creative drama for many years, this comes naturally to me. It may not be your way. However, I believe you, the zambuk, might provide a pointer in the right direction by sharing a story of your own power-out-of-weakness. This will address the balance of power and help the survivor to see you as a real person with joys and sorrows like them. If the survivor is in group therapy or a support group, they may be hearing many too many stories of powerlessness from other survivors. This can recycle the pain and enforce their own weakness. The Gospel—good news—that opens St. Mark's story of the ministry of our Lord Jesus Christ is that the powers of this world can do nothing before God's almighty grace and love. The only possible response to the devil's invitation is love. The fear of a Goliath, a Hitler, or a Lady Macbeth is their own immortality.

With the love and support of my pro-survivors, with the memories of who I really am ringing in my ears, I was able to write that first letter to my dad, confronting him with the abuse. Two days later, with another little push from a zambuk story, *The Color Purple*, I was able to mail that letter. Confronting the abuser, even if he or she is dead, is *sometimes* a wonderful way to move us along out of the wilderness of weakness and despair. However, this must be *our choice* and no one else's, and there are as many different ways of doing this as there are survivors. We can only do it when we feel powerful enough and not before. Should you, the zambuk, suggest it? Maybe—in a very round-about way. Your survivor may react very strongly, saying, "No, I could never do such a thing," but at least you have planted the seed.

I suppose the Psalms contain all that there needs to be said about the feelings involved in the struggle between God's power and our own weakness. To pray with Psalm 27, 62, 129 (almost any of the Psalms) will quiet the fears of all survivors and zambuks alike. The means of grace are byways of mystery—not always the straight path—so this confrontation may have its seeds in the power we felt in childhood. In telling my own childish "Moment of Being," in a distant mirror I see the little girl who became the woman who felt powerful enough to write that letter to her father.

A wonderful moment of power for me was when I was about eight or nine years of age and my mother and I had two tickets in "the gods" for an operetta on the life of Franz Schubert, played by a touring company. The "sold out" signs meant that complimentary tickets were not being honored that night, so the manager (in those days resplendent in full evening dress) directed us to the box office and the long line. As I stood agitatedly waiting (probably on one foot!), the overture already being played, I knew *I must go to the theater* that night. When we finally reached the man behind the little booth, it was explained that only two seats were available in the whole theater, in a box, at the price of two guineas each. This was the amount my father gave my mother for food each week for the entire family, so it was out of the question. Suddenly it felt like a life-and-death matter to me, and I staged the most wonderful temper tantrum. Sarah Bernhardt could do no better! The manager and the man in the box office conferred together, and, as the red plush curtain rose on Act I, my mother and I were escorted to our seats in the box *for free!* I sat there in a daze of wonder and ecstasy. I believe at that moment I decided that acting was for me. I feel powerful in the theater. Brother Timothy, who was my spiritual director for several years, contrasted my behavior when I was setting up my props and organizing the chapel for my performance of *Julian* at the monastery and the stories he was hearing of the tentative way I dealt with other areas of my life.

In the parable of the lost coin, the woman acts decisively and powerfully to retrieve her loss: she lights a lamp, shining it in all the dark corners of the home, and sweeps out the house, searching for it diligently everywhere. If she has wept and blamed herself for the loss of the coin, these tears must now be put aside in order to move around the furniture, crawl under the bed, shine a light in to the cupboards, throw out a mountain of old no-longer-usable stuff. This process is indeed a reordering that only realization of the loss will ensure. Notice too that it is a *woman* who loses money, not a man, and money equals power, especially for women who in every age have found themselves with less than men. In another story from the Gospels where money is involved (and there are a great many!), it is a *widow*, not a poor man, who offers her two little mites to the temple coffers, giving power to God. I am not alone as an adult survivor who has terrible problems with money, and often the only way I knew to deal with it was through a two-year-old's behavior. Car insurance money has kept me worried and awake for years and brought out the most hysterical behavior. I just cannot manage money at all. When things got out of control in one bank, I simply moved my account—but not before an awful scene with the bank managers, who asked me incredulously whether I had ever balanced my checkbook. (No, never.). I have gotten to a point in my life where I do now write down my checks most of the time, but I still believe there is a manager in white tie and tails who will whisk me away to the best seats in the house for nothing if only I plead with him! Needless to say, I have never charged the "right amount" according to worldly standards for my shows. I do all right with women and poor monks, where we understand that the rewards of found coins do not always come in monetary ways. I always give to beggars in the street if I have it on me, and I try to ask their names or offer to go with them for a sandwich, which makes us both feel better about the balance of power.

This is part of the climax of the tale of the lost coin: the woman goes to her friends and neighbors and says, "Rejoice with me. I have found that which I lost." Notice that she must have told them about the loss in the first place but did not tell everyone or make it public knowledge. This stage in recovery involves a few selected and trusted people (not "family," you will note, but "friends and neighbors"—zambuks). Later in the toad stage, your survivor may come to a place where they have to repeat the story of the abuse over and over to all. Now, in confessing the precious loss to a few she knows will rejoice when she recovers, she is slowly gaining power. We do not hear that these friends and neighbors joined in the search.

Likewise, in the parallel story for men of the lost sleep, the shepherd goes out on his own, leaving the ninety-nine in the fold, to seek for his loss. For men, this is a profound story: a hero's journey, very "au courant" in these days of greater consciousness of the male psyche. Men have more counting to do: one hundred sheep are lost, only ten coins. When I act out these parables, I make the ten coins the woman's dowry that she wears around her head as a sign that she is wife and mother and therefore a person to be accounted for. One man, a writer and university faculty member, responded:

THE LOST COIN

Being a man, he sincerely expects life to be logical. The lamb that's lost will cry and tell me where it is, he says. Being a man, he goes forth, confident, dry-eyed, listening for the lamb's plaintive bleat.

Being a woman, she sees no logic in life's losses. Only a bearing down, malevolent and cruel. Something she owns is lost. One more resource has been taken from her, and she is being pushed toward emptiness, the vast dark void that swallows women's worth. Being a woman, she grabs a broom and jabs at emptiness with quick, decisive thrusts, even as her lips frame muted words of prayer. Being a woman, she can construct her own vision of peace, a view of retrieval and renewal.

She can imagine a brightness brighter than gold—a glittering emergent hope coming forth from the darkness, arising like a joyous exalta-

tion of larks. We will rejoice, she says. My
friends and I will rejoice when that which was
lost is found.

—Clifton Anderson, 9/16/86

And I wrote this poem:

THE LOST COIN—
On discovering the truth of my terrible loss, after
the weeping,
before the lighting of a lamp, the purgation of the
busy broom,
I discover my terrible gain: *I blame myself for
this loss.*

Perhaps the father did too:
"I shouldn't have let him go off like that—so
young.
I ought to have thrown a party, killed the kid
goat."
And the shepherd:
"Maybe I didn't close the door of the fold.
I should have taken better care of *that* one."
(God forgive us—we used to call her "the black
sheep.")

But with children, we can beg their forgiveness
with fatted calves
and new shoes, with robes and with rings—
We can leave the dancing and singing, and go
outside to entreat him
to come in—And with sheep?
"He laid her on his shoulder and brought her
home, rejoicing."

But a coin?
How to forgive something as abstract as money?
Or is it?

Ask the widow, struggling to make it alone.
Ask a woman on welfare with five children to
    support.
Ask the rich suburban housewife, addicted to
    shopping.
Ask me—"Roberta, whose image is stamped on
    your coin?"
And I weep, and turn it over in my hands.
Peering through the darkness of my tears, I see,
    not Caesar, but Christ.
So I light a lamp to see him more clearly,
I take a broom to sweep through the dark and
    dusty corners of my soul;
And my home is different now—
I've thrown out some outworn furniture,
I've rearranged, I've changed, I've cleaned.
I've found what I had lost and I rejoice—*I forgive
    myself.*
And I write this poem to share with you, my
    friends and relatives.
               —Roberta Nobleman, 9/17/86

If you are on the sidelines of both these stories, as friends and neighbors of the ones with the loss, you know that this is a journey that can only be made by the "lossee," herself or himself. It is a very lonely journey. Only I can learn to balance my checkbook. Only I can truly know what to throw out, what to keep from my precious personal things. And only you as the good, kind "nurse" to the two-year-old know that when the child falls she must pick herself up again.

At this fragile stage, we can only name the mighty lion and tame it enough to "let go and let God" move us onto the great turning point: the red-hot iron. Who can we take with us as companions at this time? From the Hebrew Scriptures, Daniel in the lion's den and Judith and Esther all tell stories attesting to God's mighty power. St. Paul, St. Agnes, and the great "order" saints like St. Ignatius, St. Dominic, and St. Francis all offer their overwhelming strength and support. In our own century, we might look to the resilience of a Martin Luther King or an Ann Frank or a Rosa Parks or a Mother Teresa to know that "we shall overcome some day."

What is the role of the *leader* when the devastation of the abuse suddenly erupts like a volcano, spilling the lava of despair, scandal, and horror over entire communities?

"A kingdom divided against itself cannot stand...it is brought to devastation" (Matthew 12:25). The "doubleness" of our humanity can cause chaos, as when the leader is required to be both pro-survivor *and* pro-abuser. Where to find the neutral space, the undivided kingdom of justice and wisdom? The weakness of someone like Pilate can cause crucifixion of the innocent, and unleash a maelstrom of despair.

"How can one enter into a strong man's house and spoil his goods, except he first bind the strong man?" asks Jesus in Matthew 12:29. The good zambuk's hands are *not* tied; they are free to wipe away tears, console, and command, through the action of the one Holy Spirit. The "goods" the leader has in her house can then be freely applied to the situation without procrastination, double talk, shilly-shallying, and all the other nonsense that often impedes the recovery process. They can be king—or queen.

Whenever Jesus was confronted with messy conflict, he always responded *immediately*, drawing upon Lady Wisdom herself to intervene. Using the language of the Enneagram, one would say that he drew on the strength of the "eight," moving to the good space of the "two," truly helping, freely concerned, just. He did not do this, as I might do, trailing a toxic agenda of my own sinfulness. This was not easy for Jesus. In the telling story of the Canaanite woman who begs Jesus to heal her daughter

(Matthew 15:21-28), he makes the journey of the prodigal son from the distant journey of "I am just a Jew for other Jews" to the home of the Father and Mother of us all. The Holy Spirit must have guided Matthew's hand to include that story in the Gospels. We are given an extraordinary glimpse into the heart of justice and wisdom.

An elderly priest told me how he dealt with an incident of sexual abuse within his parish. The moment he heard of it, he brought the entire family to the rectory, and using the sword of justice, the breastplate of righteousness, the helmet of salvation, like a prince, he directed the ensuing battle until, through tears, rage, accusation, and denial, he was able to discern the still, small voice of Truth.

Before turning to red-hot iron, leaving the four animals I spent the day with at the Bronx Zoo, I want to describe one last experience: a magnificent lion and lioness basked in the winter sun, wonderful to behold when not in a cage. Reading the plaque, I discovered that this is what lions do most of the time, even in the wilds of Africa. If lions spend most of their time resting and sleeping and hunt for their prey only when necessary, if the rhythm of their lives is feast or fast, then maybe the image of the lion should be holding fast to the power of *that* reality and not the snarling, rampant, angry lion that appears on coats-of-arms and gateways to grounds houses. When Jesus was asked about a powerful demon that seemed impossible for the disciples to control (after the Transfiguration), he responded that this kind only came out through prayer and fasting.

hold
me fast

don't
let me
pass

V THE RED-HOT IRON:

RAGE—OUTRAGE AND IN-RAGE

Why, in the middle of the holding process, are we suddenly jolted out of the world of flesh-and-blood animals into the elements? Red-hot iron? Janet is now contending for the first time with something not created by God but human-made, and it is hot stuff. Cold iron may be fashioned into bars for a cage or a prison, into a sword or shackles, into an armored tank or a machine gun, but the poem speaks of red-hot iron. What does this mean at this stage? Red-hot iron brings to mind the fiery pits of the blacksmith or the witches' cauldron or the brand used for cattle, convicts, and concentration camp victims. Prince Bismarck in 1902 spoke of "blood and iron" for his military prowess. I do not like this symbol. Like Janet, I recoil in horror and fear. No wonder Tam Lin cries out so passionately,

"Hold me fast, don't let me pass, I'll cause no hurt or harm!" I do not believe him.

At the end of my show on abuse at Hartford Seminary, wearing my True Self mask, I asked a woman in the front row to help me light my candle, symbol of Hope. "I can't," she whispered to me. "I'm afraid of fire. My mother burned my fingers with matches as a child!" I lit the candle myself and whispered back to her, "Would you help me hold the candle?" "Yes," she said with tears in her eyes, and behind the mask, tears of rage at her mother sprang to my eyes too. As I turned my back on the audience to take off the mask, red-hot iron within my soul warmed and energized me through and through. "No, never again!" I vowed and turned back to face the audience for our closing ritual.

The turning point of this whole healing journey may be that "those who sit in darkness and in the shadow of death fast bound in misery and iron" may suddenly discover the release of rage at God, and at the world, that will lead them beyond the self-pity, self-hatred, and self-rage that the mighty lion imposes. Without the intervention of the red-hot iron, the suppression of the rage and fear (which often takes the form of polite, bland conversation, because to touch on serious issues would open a can of worms!) may mean the whole process is doomed to stagnation. We are all deathly scared of what lies like dross at the bottom of our souls. In our Western tradition and in our churches, the cool voice of reason and science has prevailed. There is a danger that this can happen even in the whole area of child abuse: if we just study all the statistics, set up another task force to explore "The Problem," keep it all abstract and in the head, then it will never descend to the heart! Wrote Alice Miller: "Now I see that each philosopher had to build a big, big building in order not to feel his pain—even Freud."

We have even ignored Jesus's angry sayings, like "Whoever harms one of these little ones of mine, it were better for them that a millstone be hung round their neck and they be thrown into the sea." An impersonal God, "immortal, invisible, hid from our eyes," is waiting to descend upon us when we have "provoked most justly thy wrath and indignation against us," as the Book of Common Prayer puts it. "God is allowed to be angry with us; we are not allowed to be angry with God" is the message we give our adolescents, and the red-hot iron stage is full of the ambivalence, the passions, and the energy of youth.

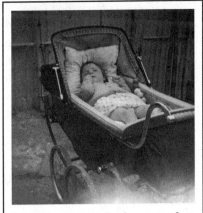

The author's sister, Jessica, at age four or five.

Let me explain what happened in my own teenage years. It will take the form of a letter. Let me not be abstract:

Dear Particular God,

I am mad as hell at you for these forty odd years of wretched, horrible insomnia that has been my wilderness, my innocent suffering, ever since Dad had his way with me as a child and then ever so lovingly put me to bed in that upper room above the shop. I remember the cars coming up over the hill on the London Road—at around three in the morning from the chiming clock—and I thought maybe I would be dead by the time they passed on down the road. I wasn't. But, I ask you, how was a child like me *supposed* to sleep at night with all those terrible feelings locked inside of her? Answer me that!

But you and I both know, God, that wasn't the worst of it. Mum and I made a pact at the age of thirteen to hang in there with Dad and not

mess up the whole family, to put it aside and pretend "it" never happened. And we did, at least
till I was sixteen and Mum got pregnant at the
age of forty-four. Another baby, yes, that would
make it all better. But you couldn't take care of
yourself, could you, Mum, and so with toxemia
and the same nasty old Dr. Ross who lanced my
abscess many years before as a child, you landed up in Pembury Hospital for close to three
months! Who took care of everything at home:
two brothers, Dad, schoolwork, trying to get into
theater school on scholarship? Me!

Was that fair, God? Jessica, the sister I
always wanted, is born severely spastic, two
months premature. The secretary calls me out of
school to say my mother is dying in childbirth.
(What about me? I need a mother too!) How I
hated that postwar hospital with its smell of
impersonal nurses, in their starched uniforms
like nasty nuns. Dad and I were "one" then in
good old Dolby spirit. We'd brave it through,
make it work, and, unlike my mother, we could
never pretend that Jessica would ever be normal.
We knew what lay ahead. So, that first
Christmas, when my mother was sent to my
grandfather's and the rest of us were left at home
with a three-month-old baby to care for, it is no
wonder that insomnia was my demon. The baby
had constant fits from the encephaloma, and the
only thing that would quiet her after all the drugs
had been given was to put her in the baby car-
riage. The cold winter air and the rocking motion
as I pounded the streets at 3:00 a.m. would eventually put her to sleep. But I was awake, and I
have been ever since.

I tell you, God, if this is your idea of a

joke...? I always say you meant me to be a Trappist nun and get up to pray at that ungodly hour, but, believe me, I wrestled with you in those awful hours. I also learned my lines for the scenes we were doing in my interrupted theater school training, and I forged forgiveness for Dad in the red-hot passion of alliance against the wife and mother who had done this thing to us. The first suicide attempt was on Christmas Day! (For God's sake, Mum, why did you always choose special occasions—Missy's birthday, Easter Sunday—to stage these tremendous "See-Me" dramas that never quite succeeded?) When I learned about it and that my beloved grandmother and my maternal great-grandfather had committed suicide too, I felt such rage and poured it all into a letter that said, "What about us? Don't we, your three remaining children, don't we matter?" I was told I shouldn't have written it (I was not allowed to be angry).

Thank you, God, for just *one* good memory of that awful time: I saw *Rebecca* with Laurence Olivier on my grandfather's brand new 12-inch black and white TV. That story sustained me through all those sleepless nights, and I vowed to myself, in secret, that I would be an actress too some day and burn down all the "Mandalays" of my imagination and claim my true inheritance with my Max De Winter (or Tam Lin). *Rebecca* was a parable for me.

Now I come to think of it, God, my Mother, you did not strike back when I raged at you. You were no weak, suicidal mother, no overworked, unfeeling doctor, and I guess you hate tumors of the brain as much as I do. I honestly don't understand the "why" of Jessica, in and out of all those institutions until she died at the age of eleven. The last time I saw her in that overcrowded mental home, cared for mostly by the Down's syndrome patients, her legs were the size of broom stick handles, and she lay in a pool of blood, as she got her period early (what irony in that?), and there was no one around to care for her, and I, her big sister, what could I do but avert my eyes and wonder about our mutual mother. She had considered putting a pillow over Jessica's face while she was sleeping as a tiny baby. Is that what *you* wanted, Big Mother God? What are we little creatures to do with such pain, such helplessness? And the way it reverberates in my ears, long after little Jessie was lain to rest in that country grave. "Of what purpose disturbing the dust on a bowl of rose leaves?" asks T.S. Eliot in "Burnt Norton." Can you tell me why I'm feeling this, God?

The tears and anger feel familiar, like writing to Dad and confronting him with the abuse. Some days later, my zambuk suggested that Jess write back to me (in my left hand). Here's the letter:

February 3, 1992

Dear Big Sister Bobbie,
Thank you for the NIGHT.
The cool winds,
The rocking—
It was *all* gift
all blessing
from God.
Without me, how could you
know for REAL how to be a
TRUE sister?

Rest is for later . . . it will come.
Your sweet
Jess Dolby

My anger is something that covers up a more basic, more spirit-filled emotion—like grief, sadness, loss, fear. I loved my mother, Jessica's mother, my father, Jessica's father, and I longed for that little sister—and to find it all so *damaged*! No wonder I feel confused about my anger! I don't really think I am a very good person to consult about anger. I know I still have "blocks" in my head that make it difficult for me to reach down to my heart and grieve—weep. We cannot *make* it happen—and anyone who grew up in the 1940s and 1950s, especially in a northern European country after a devastating war, will understand my predicament and not chastise me for failing to unearth all the repressed tears. My friend Anne expresses this so sincerely:

> We can all be mirrors for each other, which, in the case of a woman's anger, means that I can listen to someone's expression of anger but I don't have to take it in; I can be a bouncing off, caring receptacle for another woman—or man. I can help the other contain his or her anger and reflect a non-anxious response, which ultimately allows the other person to move beyond the anger.

How to be a sister, a true sister or brother to those we love? Is this the great brotherhood/sisterhood that we all long for so desperately in this violent, unkind world? The adolescent stage of anger requires a sibling response (as we often refuse to listen to our "elders and betters"), but a wise sister, a good brother is the best zambuk at this time. Writing that letter to God, I feel as though I am facing a great lake of cold, icy water, standing on the brink, too fearful to plunge in, and suddenly, I have the energy to *do it*! Tam Lin is right: the water is not so bad once we are in.

Christ will cause us "no hurt nor harm" and will swim beneath us like a marvelous fish until we reach the other side (to be greeted by a chorus of toads?!).

As I read over that letter, I realize that I went through many of the feelings of most of the Psalms! Some, like Psalm 88, leave us down in the pit, cowering before God's wrath, but most of the angry laments come to a place of healing by the end. Psalm 89 begins: "I will sing of thy steadfast Love, O Lord, forever." It is as if God reached in and pulled the poor soul out of hell by the time the next Psalm came around. Is God, in effect, ever angry with us, or do we just project our anger onto God? Julian of Norwich says, "I saw full surely that wherever our Lord appears, peace reigns and anger has no place. For I saw no whit of wrath in God." Or paraphrased by J. Janda in the play I perform on Julian:

> *Grounded*
> *in*
> *God where*
> *only*
> *mercy and*
> *ruth*
> *can grow*
>
> *neither*
> *wrath*
> *nor anger*
> *root*
> *here, nor*
>
> *blame to*
> *us*
> *who slowly*
> *grow*
>
> *in a medley*
> *of weal and woe*

I have argued with Julian for the past ten years or so on this point, and perhaps my red-hot iron can help me to understand her a little better in this extraordinary assertion. Just as the red-hot iron is made by human hands from God's substance, fire and metal, so is our anger a very special important part of our humanity, but unlike goodness or power or mercy or love, it is *not* a property of God, the Ground of our Being. God gets angry with us, but God is not an Angry God. I, as a parent, may scream out in anger to my child, "Don't ever cross the road in front of a truck again!" but that does not make me a Mean, Mad Mother. Sometimes, as Jesus showed us so clearly, anger is the only way to speak of "the candor born of anguish and passion" (Walter Brueggemann). If you are being sister or brother to an angry, passionate survivor, then to read Julian of Norwich at this time may be the best that you can do for both of you as you hear:

"I will never, never forgive him!"

"I hate her with a passion that is burning me up!"

"God, you abandoned me just when I needed you. I don't trust you. I don't like you!"

"Go to hell, God!"

"I want her to suffer like I suffered, and I want to watch it all happening!"

Is it any wonder that cursing—especially words such as "f—" and "shit" (with sexual connotations) and "God damn it!" or "Jesus Christ!"—are heard a lot more than before when all that anger was repressed? If Jesus were alive today, instead of using "Woe unto you," would he perhaps say something closer to, "F— unto you"? I don't know the word for "woe" in Aramaic, but my guess is that it probably begins with a good explosive consonant like an "F." As a Jew, Jesus inherited thousands of years of tradition at cursing and lament. The great invectives against incest are found in the last chapters of Leviticus. They may not suit our twentieth century family life, but they are there. (Could you read them, ponder them, and if possible, preach on them?)

For the church of the twenty-first century, we are in desperate need of symbols powerful enough to depict the horror of child abuse and break through the wordy denial. Let me suggest a few, many of them old symbols that have fallen into decay, and some of them new.

Jesus's whip of cords used in the cleansing of the temple is one such symbol. But let me preface this whip with the one that was used on Jesus himself at the scourging before his crucifixion. We cannot see one whip without holding up the other. In the recitation of the rosary, the scourging at the pillar is one of the sorrowful mysteries, and maybe we need to include the other whip, for that too is a sad mystery. Angry hands whipped him, ugly mouths spat upon him, cruel cords bound him, and red-hot iron was cooled to become the nails that would wound him, the sword that would pierce his side. What can whipping teach us?

When I arrived at St. John's version of the cleansing of the temple in my spiritual exercises with Sister Agnes, I had a terrible time with the words, "And making a whip of cords, he drove them all with the sheep and the oxen out of the temple" (John 4:15). John places this cleansing right after the joyous experience of the wedding at Cana, and it appears that Jesus's family may well have witnessed this, for we know from St. Luke that it was the family custom to go up to Jerusalem every year for the feast of the Passover. So imagine yourself as Mary or a relative or a disciple, seeing Jesus fashioning the whip with great intentionality, pouring out the coins of the money changers, and overturning the table of the pigeon sellers too. Can you see the cages, the iron barred doors loosened, the birds flying free? It is a magnificent picture, and a far cry from "gentle Jesus, meek and mild" or those incredibly wimpy pictures of Jesus with neatly combed blondish hair and a simpering expression that are often found on holy cards and the walls of churches. If Jesus could fashion himself a whip, so can we. Is it a dangerous thing to assume that Jesus' anger might also be appropriated by us? Indeed, but that is where "the adolescent" needs a firm hand and where you, the zambuk, need to know your part in the catharsis. Remember:

- Jesus *chose* to do this at a certain time, when the place was thronged with people for Passover, when the anger was

hot enough, when he himself felt strong enough physically, emotionally, and spiritually, and when he was certain
enough about his support group (the disciples).

- He *chose* only that part of the temple that needed cleansing. He did not go into the Holy of Holies or the women's
  section or up on the pinnacle or the part where he had daz-
  zled the scribes and learned men years before at the age of
  twelve.
- He did not use the whip on himself, the priests, the
  Pharisees, the disciples or his family. He goaded the
  sheep-and-oxen keepers outside the temple, which was
  just what they needed: to move beyond the little, petty
  power-mongering of their daily routine. Likewise, the
  pigeon sellers and money-changers were never the same
  after feeling that whip.
- He *dropped the whip* when it was over and "when evening
  came, they went out of the city " (Mark 11:19). He left.
- He identifies with the temple as his own body (John 2:21)
  and in Mark's Gospel laments that it has become a "den of
  robbers." It is the loss of what is holy and sacred in the
  hands of those who neither care nor understand the true
  sacrifice that God requires.

From the point of view of a dramatist, it seems as if Jesus was
almost putting on a show—director, chief actor, scene designer,
and property master all in one. The same is true for the drama of
the Last Supper, when again he sets the scene, calls in the chorus
and principals, and then becomes chief actor and director.

You, the zambuk, are in the position of witness to all of this.
At this stage, many survivors may not feel ready to take up the
red-hot iron for themselves or to fashion a whip. For this we need
an advocate, one who stands in for the spirit of Christ in action in
the world. I believe this to be something of my own calling. A
survivor wrote to me after seeing my show:

"You have given me something to strive for. I have just
emerged on the other side of what I fondly refer to as my *rage
phase* in which, by way of fire fantasies, I have incinerated a life-

time of accumulated dirt in the form of resentment, anger, hatred. There is the sense that this has been some kind of purification process. I feel purged of something filthy, something that ruins everything it touches."

Who or what can lead us in this priestly function? It ought to be in our churches and synagogues, but the "temple" may be found almost anywhere. When you sense there is deep anger in your survivor like a tooth that needs root canal or gums with advanced periodontal disease, you will need a specialist to "have it all out"—deep drilling, cutting, cleansing—and the whip is one of the tools carefully applied by someone who knows what they are doing. The best you can do is sit by in the waiting room.

As I look back on my own times of purification, I can say with the psalmist, "Purge me with hyssop," and know it for cleansing, not punishment. "If you will, you can make me clean," said the leper to Jesus. "I believe. Help thou my unbelief," said the father with his epileptic son after the disciples had failed to cure him. "If I only touch the hem of his garment..." said Flo, and you had better believe that twelve years of incompetent and expensive doctors must have led that lady to a place of passion and rage that only Jesus could calm. This was no shaky hand that sought out the healing power, though the Gospels tell us she trembled and fell at Jesus' feet *after* the cure—but that I understand as "fear of the Lord, the beginning of wisdom."

My greatest act of passion and rage in this stage of the journey was after I discovered that Dad had tried to rape my daughter. Without telling anyone I was going to England, I simply announced to my family in the U.S. that I needed a few days off, and I landed on my parents' doorstep out of the blue. My anger took me there—it was hardly a fairy tale reconciliation—but I managed to tell my brothers about the abuse, and I believe it set the stage for the healing that was to come in the future.

My anger at that time felt like a fire inside me. I wanted to burn things—not just for myself, but for the whole world. I understood the Greek myths and I wanted to *rage* at the gods. This was a holy anger. In the Oedipus legend of the ancient

Greeks, the Oracle foretells Laius (the father) and Jocasta (the mother) that they will have a child who will kill his father and marry his mother. The Christian response to the oracle of murder and incest is surely anger: "Hell, no! We will *not* abandon this child to the fates! Our love is stronger than death, greater than 'the Oedipus complex'! Our son belongs to a God who loved his/her Son to resurrection."

When my father received the letter confronting him with the abuse, his first response was to go up to the attic, where I kept my letters and papers and things from before my marriage, bring all of it down to the bottom of the garden, and make a bonfire of it all! My mother was the zambuk to him then, for I remember that she told me she watched him from the back door with a kind of neutrality—even amusement!

Is the whip of cords ever to be found in the hand of the zambuk? Must zambuks always accept, with docility, the projections the survivor might vent upon them? Sometimes. We may ask ourselves, after an angry outburst, "What in the life and history of this person is being played out through me, and am I able to deal with it right now in my life?" After all, you are not being paid to accept all this abuse and to calmly reply in pseudo-therapeutic tones, "Now I understand that you are feeling angry. You have a right to your rage, and I am here to be your whipping boy (or girl) if that's what you need to do." The most healthy thing to do is to state your own feelings quite truthfully: "I've had a bad day, too. I really can't handle this right now." And sometimes, when your survivor is acting like a spoiled-rotten adolescent, a burst of anger on your part may be just what is needed, especially if you yourself are feeling manipulated. The best thing a friend did for me was an enormous row we had at a Chinese restaurant. It continued into the parking lot, with his yelling obscenities over the roofs of several cars and then driving away in a fine fury. It was truly a cleansing experience for me. Coming at the right time, it helped to move me on to the next stage. The following year, around the time of the toads, we had an anniversary dinner at the same Chinese restaurant and laughed incredulously at our red-hot iron row!

The discipline—whip of cords—that was part of the monastic tradition for hundreds of years, usually applied on Fridays especially by penitential orders like the Trappists, now lies a forgotten relic in the bottom of the chest of drawers of many convents and monasteries. Many of us now view it as a masochistic, even sadistic rite. But before we discard something that served a purpose for such a long time, let us take a closer look. A whip, a belt, a cane were considered an essential part of the education of children, slaves, and servants until very recently. As a child, I was beaten in school, and at my first teaching job in Aberdeen, Scotland, I was issued a belt. All the teachers in Scottish high schools placed them on the desks before they began class in the 1950s and 1960s. Maybe you yourself have memories of childhood beatings, this being the rule, rather than the exception in "the good old days."

If violence was part of the scenario for either of you, claiming and acclaiming the rage for this is essential, and now is as good a time as any to do it. After my show, a man told how his mother beat him regularly at least five times a week, leaving welts and bruises. "I didn't mean to break the jar of mayonnaise. I hate her for what she did, but I also love her," he said. As a sister, I cried out for his pain—and for his mother's, for who knows what despair may have been visited on this poor black woman, someone's maid perhaps, for whom the jar of mayonnaise was a breaking point? We shared something so deep when he hugged me afterwards that tears of joy are filling my eyes as I write of it. "Blest be the tie that binds," says the old hymn, and it continues, "we share our mutual woes, our mutual burdens bear; and often for each other flows the sympathizing tear."

Jesus's whip is *outrage*, not *in-rage*, and this public ritual for what he must have suppressed on previous visits to the temple is an example for the church that will cause "no hurt nor harm." Alice Miller asks us if the routine and accepted "spare the rod, spoil the child" mentality that formed both Nazis and Allies as children were held up to public scrutiny, would we have had World War II? If we can know that when an innocent child like the boy who broke the mayonnaise jar and his abusive mother are the same Christ who whipped up a frenzy in the temple and a little while later felt those cords of shame himself, holding up on high this great *symbol* of purgation and pain, then perhaps we can envision a world where all whips and scourges, even for animals (especially for animals), will be laid to rest. Therapists suggest that if a person needs to lash out in anger, they find a safe place and a safe person to be with them.

I believe Jesus's whip of cords takes us beyond psychology into another realm, making our anger sacred and cleansing within the temple itself, taking it out of the private realm into the public domain where it truly belongs. Can you imagine on Holy Innocents Day if all the "Rachels" of this world were invited to the cathedral or the synagogue for a Ritual of Public Outrage at all the child abuse of this world? See it: hymns specially written, liturgical dances of grief and anger, and the leaders of churches— bishops, priests, nuns, monks—in an act of penance for the thousands of years of silence and denial, making a whip of cords and lashing out at pillars, stone altars, floors, singing a great litany of woe and weeping. What an example for our youth that would be!

One Ash Wednesday, I complained that my fourteen-year-old daughter did not wish to come to church that day. Some months later when we were laying new carpet in her bedroom, I discovered beneath a rug what looked like a bunch of burn marks on the old carpeting. She explained that her Ash Wednesday ritual had been to write down all her sins, burn them on the floor in her bedroom, and then stripping off naked, smother herself in the ashes and dance all her anger into the carpet. After a warm shower and a long jog, she was ready for Lent! And her mother had expected her to kneel for that tame little black smudge in a boring old Episcopal service!

A feminine symbol that has fallen into neglect since the nineteenth century made it into a pernicious piety is *the sword that Simeon prophesies will pierce Mary's heart.* Why pernicious? The phenomenon of the "piercing" that innocent people, particularly females and children have received at the hands of the lord of the manor, the slave master, the cruel teacher, resulted in the "suffering angel in the house" syndrome. We are still recovering from the damage this has done. Mary has her Victorian counterpart, the martyr mother. (Caruso was the seventeenth and only surviving child of his mother. Can you imagine those sixteen pregnancies?) Think of the pious virgins, young nuns who died in the cholera epidemics of cities like Chicago, Pittsburgh, Louisville, perhaps one or two survivors from an original band of thirty sisters.

This idea of the sacrificial lamb is still with us: it is a privilege to suffer. Is this only a Catholic thing? No. Good Protestant ministers were perfectly happy to let ten-year-old chimney sweeps languish in dirt and soot and misery, as long as the fires burned brightly in the manse or the rectory. Slave owners sat upright in their pews on Sunday mornings while the slave boy waited respectfully at the church door, listening to such hymn verses as "The rich man in his castle, the poor man at his gate, God made them high and lowly and ordered their estate," from the second verse of "All things bright and beautiful." Did Mary embrace her sword knowing that as "the lowly handmaiden" this was her lot in life? We know she pondered all this in her heart. We know that a sword literally pierced Jesus's side and that Mary must have witnessed this. But what of the *symbolic* sword prophesied by Simeon? Why didn't Joseph share in this sword piercing? Is it only the mother who suffers so? How can this apply to us, nearly 2,000 years later, especially if we are men who can never experience labor, birthing, nurturing within our physical selves? Can we use the word "mother" as Simeon uses the word "sword" or as Jesus uses the word "Father"—something much deeper, broader than mere gender?

Mary's sword invites men, and male priests and ministers in particular, to be mother *and* father, holding up this precious sword of truth for all the church to see. In presenting child sexual abuse to the world and to churchgoers who are heavily into denial, our leaders, enraged and outraged when they hear such stories, can brandish this sword as a healing instrument to cut through the myriad layers of sin and longing that lie beneath the act. A bishop who truly cares will listen to many survivor stories, go himself to visit the child molester in prison, and come back to the diocese to write and preach and exhort the people to pay attention to this vast injustice.

A sword always has two edges. Remember the reputation of the nice visiting uncle or good old Bob, Ann, or Bill. The public persona of the perpetrator is often impeccable. This creates a split in the mind–set of the abuser, who will rationalize: a) since it is secret and private, it is safe; b) my mask of Mr. Nice Guy or Perfect Parent and my faithful observance of church and society rules are a cover-up; c) since the victim is "mine," I may do as I please. Mary's sword can dissect through all this, separating sheep and goats in the name of justice and truth in spiritual ways that go far beyond mere legalism or even the good intentions of psychology.

One other aspect of the sword that pierces to the heart of the matter is the invitation to mysticism that the *good* aspect of nine-teenth century veneration suggests: the ecstasy and agony of Newman or St. Thérèse of Lisieux. An earlier saint, Big Teresa (of Avila), has helped me to understand this, and she surely felt that red-hot iron in her description of the sword of passion that pierced her heart. From the moment we are separated from God at birth, our cosmic memory is obliterated, and yet we have this longing for unity. Sexual orgasm ("le petit mort" or little death) is perhaps the only glimpse of heaven we mortals experience this side of eternity. The compulsive and urgent longings of the perpetrator "to make it hurt so good, baby," as the rock song puts it, are for the ecstasy of Mary's sword.

In these days of thrusting energy (the sword) and deep and terrible emptiness that must be filled somehow (the heart), you, the zambuk, might consider finding good, acceptable, safe public places to experience this. Go to the opera and choose a nine-teenth century Mary's sword-story (practically all Puccini, most Verdi, much Wagner) or experience a live rock concert. You may be the oldest person there, but no matter, undulate to U-2 or "die" with the Grateful Dead. There has to be something there to attract so many millions. Buy tickets for the Super Bowl or get the last seats for the hottest game in town. Dance, swim, ski, hike over mountains, take in worship at some church that's the opposite of yours. Gospel singing at First Baptist, a Russian Orthodox Easter, even a Billy Graham rally may all catch you up in the collective unconscious desire for red-hot iron ecstasy. Notice these are all, at this stage, *public* events. Private rage rituals come later.

When can the church elevate Mary's sword? Candlemas— the purification of the Blessed Virgin Mary and the presentation of Jesus Christ—is a very old festival that fell out of favor in these later days. A ceremony with candles and swords in every church throughout the land six weeks after Christmas Day—can you imagine it? What a preparation for Lent that would be, and what an Epiphany too.

A closure for this ritual should be a great singing of Simeon's exultant Nunc Dimittis. We forget, so familiar with this great song of freedom, that it is essentially the ecstatic uttering of a slave to his master. Bonds have been broken, and a new age is seen on the horizon. Flo, leaving behind twelve years of servitude to her bloody issue, hears Jesus's final words ringing in her ears: "Go in peace." The Gerasene man with multiple personality disorder has broken the fetters of fury for the last time and now sits clothed and in his right mind; Jairus's daughter is calmly eating her dinner that night after her death-like experience; Lazarus is folding his shroud; Mary is wrapping her baby in swaddling bands; Teresa of Avila's butterfly emerges from the cocoon to stretch fragile wings; and in my poem, Janet dips her beloved Tam Lin, first in a bowl of milk, and then in a bowl of water. This is a "light to lighten the Gentiles, and a glory to God's chosen people, Israel." This is a pure, white, peaceful place.

The bowl of water is surely the great weeping that was to follow the presentation in the temple —with the slaughter of the Holy Innocents. We can all pray for the gift of tears and for the gift of the milk of kindness. Now is a good time to *begin* to set up boundaries and caretaking. After the deluge, after the fires have finished smoldering within us, is a good time to mother ourselves. We may have "to go to Egypt." Where is "Egypt" for you? For Mary and Joseph, their refuge was a place where their forebears had suffered and died—yet this was safe and Nazareth was not.

For me, Holy Cross Monastery has been "Egypt." I could not have done what needed to be done at home. I also needed to do it alone, but with a "safe" community of men. Mother's milk and water will vary according to the body of your anger. Medieval people believed that our temperament was governed by the fluids in our bodies: melancholy, sanguine, phlegmatic, and choleric. I think they were on to something. There is a physiological basis to why some people express more anger than others. We would now label the phlegmatic person "passive-aggressive" and say that the choleric one "has a right to her rage."

Mary's sword. We can trust it when it is held in the hands of a good angel. The loving kindness of this angel will be especially careful with religious language at this stage. Relating to God our Father may be impossible for one who has been violated by a father. Tell survivors to confess all their anger to a male priest (also called "father") and they will take the sword and bludgeon you over the head! Jesus, our brother, may be a beautiful idea unless your experience of brother has been abusive. Even the word "brotherhood" is enough to elicit great snorts of fury!

If mother was your perpetrator, then your anger at the Mother Church, Mother Mary, or Mother God may be at its zenith. A big sister who failed to protect her little brother will not be imaged well in the story of Martha and Mary. "How come Lazarus was so lucky? I had no sisters to cry over me!" they say. For the survivor to hear the story of Lot's virgin daughter being sacrificed to the rapists; or Ishmael and Hagar being abandoned by Abraham and Sarah to death in the desert; or Joseph being thrown into the pit by his brothers; or for the survivor to read John Donne ("Batter my heart, three-personed God...except thou ravish me") can elicit red-hot rage. Who needs a "ravishing God"? John

Donne, maybe—but not I. To chastise the person for "radical feminism" or "disobedience" will only heat up the brand.

Between Bethlehem and Egypt is the great wilderness of Sinai, and Herod's sword sent the Holy Family there. Mary's sword sustained them in the desert and Simeon must have realized that this was the first glimpse of light for Gentiles, as he pondered his prophecy back home in Jerusalem.

A third symbol is already with us in many churches: Corpus Christi, *the naked body of Christ on the cross,* often presiding over the well-fed and overdressed priests. Isn't it ironic that we celebrate the great symbol of Christ's body, in bread, held in the hands of the priest who adds *extra* clothing (the chasuble) while Jesus was stripped of his garments? I saw a film last night on TV about Hinduism. The holy men were totally naked, covered only by the white neutralizing powder that signifies death to "self" (as does a white-faced clown in our own Western world). They purified themselves in the River Ganges at the sacred city of Benares. Contrast that with a meeting of bishops in Rome or Canterbury, clad in rich robes, following a jewel-encrusted cross as they march in single file into the palaces and cathedrals! From the point of view of survivors, living with memories of pants pulled down and little nightgowns pushed up, we identify with the holy Hindus more readily than the robed and mitered Christians.

Is Corpus Christi only a little white wafer trapped in a gold monstrance? In medieval times, the great pageants of the church were celebrated on that day in every city and village in Europe, not by the priests, but in the dramas enacted by fishmongers, shoemakers, and seamstresses—the mystery plays. It is in one such play that Mary, the mother of Jesus, remonstrates a Roman soldier on Holy Innocents Day: "If any one of you dares to touch this child of mine, I'll slit his throat!" Now, that is the spirit of Mary's sword that we need today, as fierce as a *good* mother bear with her cubs! What can we do to bring back this warm and protective care that exposes the cruelty of child abuse to the full light of common sense?

I performed in St. Johns, Newfoundland, Canada, a city that

has been plagued recently with a spate of child sexual abuse cases within the church, a blessed wound that is still bleeding and sore. The Basilica at St. Johns is a great Romanesque style structure reflecting the power and magnificence of former times. The church militant and triumphant is ill-equipped to deal with poor, lonely, frustrated Christian Brothers and child-victims. The reality of Christ's sweating, bloody, broken, naked body, his circumcised penis (as "King of the Jews") fully exposed to the jeering crowds, the women at the foot of the cross, cannot be countenanced. Our ideas of "decency" deem it necessary to cover his shame with a neatly folded loincloth. Yet the hands and the heart of Jesus are raised up for adoration.

I do not know how these symbols can be incorporated into twenty centuries of denial by the church without creating terrible chaos and offense in ordinary, well-meaning people. This has been a problem for artists of all kinds when approaching religious subject matter, particularly in matters of sexuality. We have devotions to every part of Jesus's body except his penis. Would we have less child abuse if every artist who came to that part of his body were given free reign to dispense with the obligatory wreath of mist or hand strategically placed? The "unseemly parts," as St. Paul describes the penis and vulva, are surely acceptable in God's sight. Both abusers and victims need to know this truth. Many men and women grow up with an abhorrence of these private parts. We have paid a terrible price for this privacy. Corpus Christi would be a good day to retrieve a more wholesome sexuality for the church. Celibacy can be a great gift in this respect when it is freely embraced and the dark side fully explored.

The zambuk might take the outraged or depressed survivor and let him or her come to know the full physical Christ in some act that publicly acknowledges our sexuality, even as they may not yet name their own private agony. What could you do to proclaim Corpus Christi today? Would gently bathing an AIDS patient in a hospital setting be healing for you? Or a gift of a beautiful nightgown or underwear or an elegant bathrobe? Or a visit to an art museum to see the *real* pictures? Or a meditation on a naked baby? Or a procession in church that includes pictures of people and places where the body of Christ is suffering badly?

All of these rituals help us to show that from the depths of our rage and anguish someone cares enough to pay attention, take us seriously, and show us kindness. The robbers stripped the traveler naked, but the good Samaritan gently covered him. The zambuk becomes a Simon of Cyrene who helped to carry Jesus's cross or a Veronica who wiped away the blood and sweat and tears. "I see your pain and anger, and I will do what ever I can to alleviate it, be it ever so small an act." This is dipping it all in a bowl of milk and then in a bowl of water.

To dig out all the anger may not be possible right now, especially if it has been carefully suppressed for many many years. But even a glimpse is a step in the right direction which needs to be applauded. All of those "woe unto you, Pharisees, white-sepulchers, blind fools, hypocrites" were a preparation for that greatest of all outcries: "My God, my God, why hast thou forsaken me?" Wet, warm anger is somehow holier, healthier, than cold, dry, sullen pouting. Litanies of cursing could be written down and brought to a sacred brazier as prayers to burn, with holy water from the font to douse the flames, incense to send the prayers to heaven, and a revival of the early Christian custom of serving milk and honey to new Christians—mother's milk. If you have ever tasted breast milk as an adult, it is thin and sweet and very digestible, just what a person needs when they are feeling spent.

For the red-hot iron we need human ingenuity, and here is where the great insights of twentieth century psychology may be especially helpful. These can become idols like everything else, and then we recycle the pain and cannot make the rage a holy thing. We stoke up the fires until we are burned to a cinder.

There is a different red-hot iron, a purification rite such as Isaiah experienced in the year that King Uzziah died (Isaiah 6): "The seraphim having in his hand a burning coal which he had taken with tongs from the altar, and he touched my mouth." Isaiah knows "he is a man of unclean lips, and he comes from a people of unclean lips." Why did ancient Greeks perform their great festivals of tragedy and comedy? Why did the lay people of medieval times drag their pageant plays around the cities of Europe, telling of Adam and Eve and Jesus and Mary? Why do crowds still throng to hear the stories of Hamlet, King Lear, and Romeo and Juliet? What is the twentieth century equivalent? Where do we go for catharsis, especially in these apocalyptic times when rich and poor, old and young, black and white, male and female seem caught up in a wheel of fire and rage at one another. Isaiah, John the Baptist, Mary Magdalene—where can they be found? I believe they live right next door, if only we seek them out. These souls can help us to move into a whole new realm where, with God, all things are possible.

A final meditation on this crucial stage takes us beyond the self to seek out fellow sufferers. The angels tell Mary Magdalene to "weep no more," and Jesus tells her to go and give the good news of the Resurrection to the disciples huddled together in grief. Such a saint will surely understand and help us through this painful time.

REMEMBERING VIRGINIA WOOLF

Oh, Virginia, was there no telling
Of the despair except to the god of the sea?
Or was there no relief in the telling
Just the pain of re-living the agony?

And why do only the agonies remain
Embedded in our flesh, branded in our brain?
Where do milder, magical moments go?
Are they destroyed through and through?

What grave tragedy of flesh and kin
At so innocent an age to be made part of sin.
The anxiety, the violation, the pain and the fright.
Where the ample loving arms to set things right?

Oh, Virginia, for all the Virginias of the world I weep.
Not safe in your own bed where do you sleep

But in the salty arms of the tide coming in.
Washed in death, sweet child, you did not sin!
—Phyllis Cardona

The following is reprinted from *morningstar adventures: women finding direction in the dawn of a new day.*

ON PREPARING THE WAY FOR THE
DIVINE CHILD
By Julie Keefer
"Create in me a clean heart, O God; renew
within me a resolute spirit."

I believe that unclaimed rage is at the heart of the violence and destruction we do to ourselves, each other, and the environment. As we allow ourselves, through grace, to work toward unburying this energy, I believe we set free the creative energies with which to create and live the lives we deeply long for.

In reflecting on rage, I believe it comes from the child's unmet and thwarted needs to assert themselves; to know themselves in relationship to the outer world. A child needs to explore boundaries and to be taken seriously as a human being with feelings and needs. The will is the vehicle for self-assertion; it is an inborn divine drive which, when handled properly with unconditional love and appropriate encouragement and guidance, learns how to channel the personality's energy in constructive and creative ways into the world. When this will to assert is seen as "evil" or "bad" and suppressed in inappropriate or abusive ways or not acknowledged and valued by attention to feelings and needs, then I believe rage develops.

Rage masks itself in "wounded" ways of exercising will; we develop elaborate mechanisms of defense and control, albeit unconsciously, with which to meet our need for affirmation, acceptance, love, etc. We deny these needs in the guise of appearing strong, put together, holy, knowledgeable, helpful, unique, powerful, beautiful, fit, creative, accomplished. When we continue to hold on to this destructive control system based on denial, we abandon our "native" selves, the self created in the image of the Divine. This abandonment of our native selves fuels rage. We may not be conscious of this rage, but it comes out in our inappropriate use of anger and aggression, active or passive, externalized or internalized. It comes out against ourselves every time we neglect our own deep need for mind/body/spirit nurturance. It also comes out against our environment with each unconscious, uncaring choice we make in using precious natural resources.

Spirituality or religion can be used by us as a way to exert "wounded" will, to control the definition of truth or reality for others and be vulnerable to hearing the truth of our own reality. We can become quite adept at disguising this control, justifying our actions as "God's will." In fact, we ourselves believe that it truly is God's will. This is the hardest reality to bring change into. It is reflected in self-righteousness and judgmentalism based on psychological projection and fear. Not until our personal world begins to crumble around us out of sheer exhaustion of trying to keep it together or due to illness or loss or addiction, do we wake up to the truth of this self-destructive control.

In denial of our true feelings and needs, we are not who we truly are. And if we will be honest with ourselves, we feel our isolation, our loneliness, our frustration, anger, and rage. If feelings and needs remain unacknowledged and shame to acknowledge them is present, we may not have the strength or courage to face this wounded will alone.

Unfortunately, illness or loss or, if we are more fortunate, the power of love is what usually wakes us up to this wounded will. As our wounded will is acknowledged, the pain of realization, which may include fear, sorrow, anger, and rage, must be fully felt and losses of unlived life grieved. As we become vulnerable and our defense system, which is a wrapping of protection for what is precious in us but denied, is slowly unwrapped to give freedom to our native selves. This is a process occurring over time and requires patience and self-compassion. Vulnerability requires trust. It requires us to feel safe enough to begin and to continue to unwrap the defenses. It takes grace, the presence of Spirit, of Love, to lead us in this unwrapping process.

Our society and world is filled with suppressed adult children exerting their "wounded" wills to get their way, to control reality in the directions they decide will ensure their survival. How desperately we all need to feel safe enough to let go of control and risk faith in something greater than ourselves, yet also within us, which can lead us in a new direction toward our native life…the life intended for us.

So what we need is grace, through faith in the forgiveness we have received through Jesus, to return to the child's wonder and awe, to their excitement for exploration, for their natural expression and reception of affection, for their need to have safe boundaries and adequate mirroring of loving, accepting caregivers. We need to open to and give attention to the Divine Child within waiting to be born. We need to take responsibility for the needs that we have and learn to receive what we need. This is what it means to re-parent ourselves, to co-create with God, to give ourselves opportunities to experience wonder and awe, the excitement of exploration, and expressions of intimacy. We need to create or find safe spaces where we know our limits, can be our authentic selves, and are able to risk trustworthy mirroring, honest feedback, from ourselves and others, with which to accept ourselves into greater possibility. To me this is what it means to be "church" to one another. It helps set us free. It helps liberate our giftedness. It helps support our creative offering to the world.

With this sense of inner and outer safety, we can continue to examine our core beliefs and our behaviors in life and see where they mask rage, where they suppress inner nativity, the birthing of wholeness, compassion, intimacy, creativity, love…the Christ life. S.I.N. (suppressed inner nativity) creates the illusion of safety and predictability in our lives…as long as we can do life on our terms. Spiritual transformation and psychological wholeness call us to face these illusions and open ourselves to life in its fullness, to both pleasure and pain. It allows us to risk becoming all we can be and doing all we are called to do; generative nativity…Christa comes!

hold me fast
me
don't let pass

VI THE TOAD:

THE COURAGE TO CHANGE AND EVEN TO LAUGH

On the Other Side of rage...
  Partnership lies in waiting
On the Other Side of rage...
  Peace with Justice is visible
On the Other Side of rage...
  Freedom knows no boundary
On the Other Side of rage...
  A song of Joy is ringing
On the Other Side of rage...
  The Hope we'd hoped renews us
On the Other Side of rage...
  A Little Child will lead us.
(By Julie Keefer, reprinted from morningstar adventures:
women finding direction in the dawn of a new day.)

If God is the one who wipes away all our tears, what transition can take us from red-hot iron to the little toad? If two sides of hope are anger and courage, what angels can accompany us to the next stage? It was Raphael who accompanied Tobias on his journey, Beatrice who monitored Dante, and Gabriel who visited Zechariah and his faithful support group in the outer part of the temple—all at prayer, waiting for a vision (Luke 1:5-24). Let us not forget his wife Elizabeth and her friends and relatives praying at home. A miracle is promised and, in the words of the angel, the mission of John the Baptist is "to turn the hearts of the parents to the children." In a kind of fairy-tale feat, Zechariah is struck dumb, and his wonderful prayer group (zambuks par excellence!) "all realize that he has seen a vision in the temple." No words are necessary. Zechariah returns home to Elizabeth and again, without the need of words, the aged couple make love and John the Baptist is conceived. Echoing Sarah, Elizabeth, finding herself pregnant after menopause, says to herself, "This is the Lord's doing! Now at last he has taken away my reproach before men!" One senses the wisdom of the older woman and the humor—she is letting go the rage of that "reproach," the shame, the blame.

A recent photo of the author with the "Innocent Child" mask.

If you are familiar with that great work on prayer, *The Interior Castle* of St. Teresa of Avila, there is a transition stage between the third and fourth mansions of the crystal castle of the soul. Janet's journey echoes the baby's within the womb: a novena, nine phases. Teresa envisions seven mansions, and both seven and nine are mystical numbers. Either way, we need an *odd* number so that there is a turning point. Teresa advises that many souls become stuck in the third mansion—and likewise in the healing journey of the survivor. I know how easy it is to be stuck in red-hot iron, caught between anger and courage—but somehow without the hope to move on towards something better. This clinging to the pain of the past points to a future that is bleak indeed.

The role of kith and kin are very much part of Sonya's last speech in Act IV of *Uncle Vanya* by Anton Chekhov:

SONYA. There is nothing for it. We must go on living! (a pause) We shall go on living, Uncle Vanya! We shall live through a long, long chain of days and weary evenings; we shall patiently bear the trials which fate sends us; we shall work for others, both now and in our old age, and have no rest; and when our time comes we shall die without a murmur, and there beyond the grave we shall say that we have suffered, that we have wept, that life has been bitter to us, and God will have pity on us, and you and I, uncle, dear uncle, shall see a life that is bright, lovely, beautiful. We shall rejoice and look back at these troubles of ours with tenderness, with a smile—and we shall rest. I have faith, uncle; I have fervent, passionate faith. (Slips on her knees before him and lays her head on his hands; in a weary voice.) We shall rest!

(TELYEGIN softly plays on the guitar.)

SONYA. We shall rest! We shall hear the angels; we shall see all heaven lit with radiance; we shall see all earthly evil, all our sufferings, drowned in mercy which will fill the whole world, and our life will be peaceful, gentle, and sweet as a caress. I have faith, I have faith (wipes away his tears with her handkerchief). Poor Uncle Vanya, you are crying. (Through her tears) You have had no joy in your life, but wait. Uncle Vanya, wait. We shall rest (puts her arms round him), we shall rest! (the Watchman taps.)

(TELYEGIN plays softly; MARYA VASSILYEVNA makes notes on the margin of her pamphlet; MARINA knits her stocking.)

SONYA. We shall rest!"

(The curtain slowly drops.)

This "curtain" is the ending envisaged for many survivors. Rage is spent, the tears are dried. The cup of milk is gulped down and we sit out the rest of this life waiting for the next. Father Richard Rohr asks, "Why, in the battle between psychology and spirituality, does psychology always win?" Is he right? Is that all there is? After reading this dreary prognosis, I take up Teresa of Avila (who surely experienced enough of life's ups and downs to qualify today for heavy-duty therapy!) and read her joyous, lively, passionate insistence on coming through the cocoon of our darkness to the light of the beautiful butterfly—and into union with "his Majesty"—Christ—our True Self.

I think of St. Paul with his rage against the early Christians, who was transformed into the wonderful warrior and mystic who could write of joy in the midst of pain and suffering and persecution.

When we have emerged from the icy waters, we may see—to our great surprise—swimming up to meet us:—a *toad*! Not a tadpole—please note—or a frog—but a fully grown toad. Says the encyclopedia:

"It would be hard to find a funnier friend than the toad. They live in our gardens, under our porches, in the fields, by ponds, and by roadside. When the toad is hurt or frightened, it ducks its head or uses its front feet to push away in annoyance, much as a person would. The toad is clumsy compared to its relative, the frog (who can hop far and fast). Like their enemies the garter snakes, toads shed their skins and then eat them. They absorb water through their skins and can change their size when they want to. Like a flicking whip, the sticky tongue of the toad darts back and forth to catch its prey. Their singing may be most melodious and it is often a forecast of rain.

The toad undergoes a wholly different type of metamorphosis from the butterfly. It comes out of the egg as a small, wriggling tadpole. The tadpole lives under water and breathes by means of gills. But as it grows larger, it develops lungs and pairs of forelegs and hind legs. Gradually, the tadpole loses its gills and tail by absorbing them into its body. A chemical substance which the tadpole secretes from a ductless gland brings about all these changes, or metamorphosis. When the tadpole is ready to leave its home in the water and live mostly on the land, the metamorphosis is finished."

And from my observations of toads at the Bronx Zoo:

"The plant-eating tadpole becomes the carnivorous toad."

"In the sexual embraces of toads, the male holds the female fast, until the eggs are laid."

Holding fast through the waiting time is an important part of the story for zambuk and survivor.

Could you think of yourself as a male toad, your survivor now ready to conceive something *new*? Like Zechariah and Elizabeth? The energy is spent—the iron is cooled and tempered. Nothing but time can turn a tadpole into a toad. (It cannot be microwaved!) Elizabeth must wait on the birth of her baby. In some of the healing stories in the Gospel, there is a sequencing, like the blind man in John 9:1-41: Jesus spits on the ground, makes mud pies, anoints the man's eyes, and tells him to wash in the pool of Siloam—and that is only the beginning of the story! A whole metamorphosis seems necessary.

Before we leave the Bronx Zoo, read:

"In the end, we conserve only what we love; we will love only what we understand; we will understand only what we are taught."

I believe this applies to the survival of every one of us on this earth.

The fairies who caught up Tam Lin as a little orphaned child—thrown to the ground (his grandfather cared for the hunt more than his grandchild!)—now demand a terrible price: "Every seven years we pay a tithe to hell." Unless Janet can hold him fast, he fears it will be himself. Many of us have fallen under that spell and believed "the bad fairies." The truth is the fairies of mere survival alone will tax us terribly, and scream in our ears, when, like Ezekiel, we opt for "a heart of flesh, not a heart of stone."

The "spells" of the twentieth century, the "fairies" with their angel-like wings and their other-worldly powers, cannot be judged or blamed—but ultimately if we open ourselves to transforming grace, that alone can bring us to "the seminary training" necessary for the future celebrant (priest). I have some idea of what takes place in the seminaries of this country, and I doubt if it has any resemblance to the metamorphosis described above— but maybe it should?

I like toads, just as I loved and still love the fairy tales that I absorbed as a child. If your ethnic origin is from Northern Europe, you probably grew up with fairies too—and there were all kinds: noble fairies like King Oberon and Queen Mab, trolls and elves of Scandinavia, banshees and leprechauns from Ireland, poltergeists from Germany, and those homey "hobgoblins" that we sang about in John Bunyan's Pilgrim hymn:

"Hobgoblin, nor foul friend shall daunt thy spirit, we know we at the end—Shall life inherit."

As a Brownie (Girl Scout) in England, we were divided into groups of six:—"fairies, imps, sprites, gnomes, and elves." I was an "elf" and this was the elf song:

"This is what we do as elves,
think of others, not ourselves."

This was the kind of message little girls received, growing up in the 1940s and 1950s. I loved being an elf, but I hated that song and made up rude words to replace the original and taught them to the rest of the elves! For this, I was thrown out of the Brownies—I remember standing outside the door of the parish hall, waiting for my friends after the denouncement, hearing them all sing "Taps" and feeling exceedingly pleased with myself!

I liked my "toads." I remember the fairy tale by Charles Perrault: There was once a widow with two daughters. The oldest—"a pert hussy"—was under the spell of a fairy, who tells her, "I give you a gift, that at every word you speak, there shall come out of your mouth a *toad*!" The youngest one—"so good, so mannerly"—was given the gift that, "at every word you speak, there shall come out of your mouth either a flower or a jewel."

My fellow celebrant, the lovely Sister Ave Clark, O.P., definitely qualifies as a younger sister! I still treasure Ave's pink silk roses which she so generously offers to other survivors at her retreats and workshops. I identify with "toad-speakers"—with the soubrette rather than the ingenue. All of my life, I have been given the role of the saucy maid, rather than the heroine. As a child, I disliked intensely stories of passive heroines like "Sleeping Beauty," "Snow White" and "Cinderella." I loved "Hansel and Gretel"—especially the part where Gretel pushed the witch into the oven. But my all-time favorite was Grimms' "Twelve Dancing Princesses." They outwitted their father, the king, and spent every night in a secret underground "heaven" with forests of gold and silver trees, a lake, and an enchanted palace, where they wore out their slippers dancing with twelve handsome princes! I sort of liked "The Frog Prince" and applauded the princess for hanging in there with the frog who sat at her plate at dinner and on her pillow at bedtime and eventually became her prince. "Beauty and the Beast" was also a favorite; I hated "Red Riding Hood," liked "The Three Bears," cried buckets over "The Little Mermaid," "The Little Match Girl," "The Ugly Duckling." I think you have the picture. What can the zambuk do for the adult-survivor-moving-into-celebrant? What do these fairy stories of dysfunctional families from "once upon a time" have to tell us? Why do the fairies change iron into toads? What spells do we use when we begin to hear things like:

"I guess now that Mom's been dead all these years, what's the use of carrying around all this rage and hatred? She had a pretty hard life herself, now that I come to think of it."

"Do you know I couldn't say the word 'incest' without choking up. Today I said to someone I didn't even know, 'Yeah, I'm a survivor of incest too,' just as casual as can be!"

"I told my supervisor today, 'You are just like my father and he abused me when I was little. I'm not little any longer and I am not taking any more of this crap!'"

Something's beginning to emerge. What does a toad-watcher do? Relax and enjoy; your work is beginning to get easier. Mercy and pity are afoot, fragile though the little toad may be. What stance to adopt? A tender, neutral, amused observation—like Jesus must have felt watching the Samaritan woman leaving the well, knowing perhaps what is ahead.

This is the time when the survivor may change therapists, file for divorce, put the kids in day care, leave a job, join a new survivor group, balance the checkbook, leave a religious order or join one, get a haircut, take up basket weaving, write poetry, do journaling. The survivor may suddenly decide to go back to school to learn Spanish, or redecorate the whole house, or conquer the fear of driving on the highway. They will even look different! There is a light in their eyes.

Remember that for this phase the celebrant-to-be is returning to the painful memories of the early eft stage and looking back at them from the perspective of the more balanced, mature toad. Memories now seem more manageable. What can help them face the consequences of embarking on this new journey? The great public rituals of the red-hot iron are now replaced with what I call "spells." When you finish this chapter, you will have your own name. A tutorial atmosphere, the shaman's cave, the quiet room in the monastery, the bathroom, the summer house in the park, the beach hut, or the only fireplace around, are all places to go for these private rituals. There may be just the two of you involved. Let me suggest a few, based on the elements earth, air, fire, water. Some of us feel more inclined to one than the others. There are people who *have* to be near water and those that must be within range of mountains, some who love flying and some who love fires and hot places. The seasons may also come into consideration—both of nature and the liturgical year of the church. The toad stage for me would be April and Advent. The elements also suggest North, South, East, and West. (where are you most comfortably headed?) and senses (earth), intellect (air), intuition (fire), and feelings (water). For yourself and your significant other, do you complement or clash with each other? To achieve balance in the relationship, we need to know and understand ourselves and one another. Kithing—the ability to become "Kith" to another—is only possible when we understand what works and what does not work for us both. And remember the transitional space between you must be honored at all times.

Earth

"My mistress when she walks, treads on the ground."— Shakespeare

• Walking of all kinds—hiking, mountain climbing, skiing— can all be made into a healing ritual. I read a beautiful letter in *Wing Span* (the newspaper of the men's movement). The author was getting in touch with his "Green Man" (one of the ancient fairy folk of Northern European mythology, fellow to Hildegard of Bingen's greening spirituality), walking his dog every day in the "wilds" of Yonkers, New York—except his Green Man was being trashed. He obediently picked up all the litter, Boy Scout style. This can make a person feel angry and "used," even when one chooses to do it. He needed a ritual to help him let go of his frustrations at the despoilers. On a warm sunny day, he picked four sprigs from a tree, stripped off naked, and lay on the earth under a tree. He then ceremoniously placed the sprigs on different parts of his body and covered himself with leaves. He then quietly dressed and went on his way. He rid himself of the demons and picked up the trash with a light heart the next day. I was deeply moved by this letter and thought how such bodily rituals as these will heal us. It seemed a manly thing to do, though it may well be appropriate for women too. I think we would need a trusting zambuk with us, and of course this is not for everyone!

• When the old memories have caused terrible bodily reactions, we may need an equally physical response. A woman with memories of oral sex with her father always wanted to throw up the semen. In a private ritual with a tender loving zambuk, she took her father's picture—and a good dose of salts—and vomited all over the photograph. Feeling much better, she and the zambuk then buried the whole sad mess under a tree.

• Likewise when the abuse has been anal (as in many homo-

A mask made by a multiple personality disorder victim.

sexual encounters), an enema can be a blessed relief. For those of us who suffer from constipation, a very common complaint for survivors of childhood abuse, especially when we have held it all in for so many years, an enema is much more satisfying than a laxative. Make the bathroom into a sacred place, as it is for many of us. I have visions of archaeologists 5,000 years from now excavating in suburban New Jersey and unearthing the sacred altars (sinks) with their "gods" of "H" and "C" and the vessels of purification (toilet bowls).

• Deep relaxation, massage, meditation, hypnosis, and yoga—these can all help us to begin to deal with long-term chronic complaints, like insomnia. This has been my "demon" for so many years. Says the poet Anne Sexton, a victim of her father's sexual abuse and who committed suicide long before she arrived at the toad stage:

> I must not sleep—
> What voyage this, little girl?
> This coming out of prison?
> God help—
> This life after death?

The efts and toads seem to crawl into bed with us for years to come. How to track them down and rest, *before* the next world? Are we doomed to toss and turn night after night, not trusting ourselves to passively accept "sleep that knits up the raveled sleeve of care," as Shakespeare (another insomniac!) put it?

• One of the ways our ancestors and ancestresses in medieval times came to terms with the fears that beset them was to face them all with a sacred mask. This photo of my mother-mask for my show on Mary (*Blessed!*) is my way of revealing the courage of Mary, who followed her son up the hill of Calvary, and then stood at the foot of the cross, looking up unflinchingly.

The author with the mask of the survivor—from *Blessed!*

Can we face our fears, and eventually let them go? Art therapy, clay modeling, quilting, sculpture, basket weaving—these are all ways to unearth the healing powers of the toad. The masks of protection described in Chapter III are wonderful to make, to help us "face it." We may want to discard the mask ("I don't need this anymore") or we may want to make new ones to help us on to the next part of the journey. Connecting with the daydreams of our childhood may help us to be grounded in this time of the toad.

I shall never forget Liza, who finally made it up the highway to my house, driving herself with her zambuk beside her. The lion-power of big trucks and high-speed travel is something frightening to many of us. Driving in a little car with a huge truck bearing down on you can be devastatingly familiar for a survivor. (I try to imagine that the truck driver is Tam Lin and the truck contains all the props and costumes for my shows, so this is beloved, not fearful.) When I heard that Liza's dream, as a child, was to be a racing driver at Le Mans, I thought that a little Gestalt-style confrontation might be helpful (and fun!). In

Gestalt, you sit "the fears" in an empty chair and then carry on a dialogue. In dialogue with Liza's demon, we unearthed a little of the understanding that may help retrieve the love that can cast out fear. We made a demon mask and then ceremoniously buried it in the garden. I have torn my own mask into shreds—and let my insomnia float down the Hudson River.

Am I sleeping better? Is Liza getting speeding tickets on Route 80? We're getting there!

• Birthday parties with hats, favors, finger food, and favorite people can be helpful, especially if you never had a birthday party as a child.

• Or try making a compost heap—and then mushing in all your memories (use biodegradable paper).

• A dear friend in the West who, when she finally wrote to her father confronting him with the abuse of her childhood, received the usual denial, took her anger and despair and literally chopped down a tree that had endangered the house, thus saving money on therapists and tree surgeons in one fell swoop! She has since held a wake for the wounded child that she was, and let that little girl part of herself go in peace. Ann has written a song for our mutual heroine, the woman with the issue of blood. It is called "Here Comes Flo!"

• Gardening, sewing, cooking, laundry, woodworking, painting, carpentry, even housecleaning can all serve a purpose. These are all pursuits where the zambuk can share, encourage, enjoy, and laugh along. When I feel "toady," I go and mess about with my props and costumes, tacking up a hem here, gluing on a piece there, and it is wonderfully calming.

• And, of course, *writing*. Someone once asked Robert Frost what was the most important thing about writing poetry and he replied: "The application of the seat of the pants to the seat of the chair." You, the zambuk, can expect poems to read, journals, essays—and sometimes even a smile.

Here's something I wrote ("Of Life and Limb") that appeared in a 1994 issue of *The Other Side* (reprinted with permission):

The call can come anytime, day or night, from Karen or Candy, Nadine or Nell: "Roberta, could you come sit for me tomorrow? I am absolutely desperate!" If I can, I come. We are not talking babysitting, house-sitting, or dog-sitting—but sitting (or standing) at the local art center for drawing classes, painting, sculpture, or, as they say, "life." "Life," for you Philistines, means sitting in the nude, the buff, the altogether—knicker-less, bra-less, skirt-less, sock-less. As I write this, in between twenty-minute poses, I am wearing my glasses...period.

What would make a nice, middle-class, suburban lady of fifty-two years, wife and mother of three, take up such a dubious line of business? As an actress, my body is my instrument—but is it meet, right, and seemly so to do?

I shall never forget the scandalized looks on my kids' faces, three years ago, when it finally dawned on them what Mom was doing on Tuesday evenings: "Oh, my God, Mom, that's so embarrassing! Don't ever tell any of my friends!" And my husband? In a marriage of nearly twenty-five years, nothing—but *nothing*—fazes my phlegmatic, congenial spouse.

What are the job requirements for this line of work? Should any of you theologians, ministers, bishops, presidents of synods, chancellors of dioceses, editors of Christian magazines, etc., be considering a little modeling in your spare time, the following are required.

The first essential is the ability to *sit still*—and enjoy it, be at peace with it. This is a rare commodity in our days of eat on the run, TV commercials, quick-shop, quick-print, quick-fix, rap songs, and disco dancing. Watch children in class, or teenagers at the mall, and you will realize that we are raising hyperactivity to the norm. One of the reasons kids don't go to church as much these days is that sitting still for an hour, even with the snack break that communion provides, is practically impossible for the poor dears. I find modeling a most contemplative experience—sitting in one position for three hours, with the orderly stretch breaks a rare luxury. The silence which often accompanies the concentration and attention of the artists allows me time to pray.

157

Sitting as naked as God made me, I can just be. By the end of many a session, I have found the answer to some problem, just by waiting on it. One of the instructors plays Bach, or soft modern jazz, in the background, so I relax and enjoy and listen. A real treat!

Second, you need *humility*. If any of my readers harbors illusions about the body beautiful, let me enlighten you—this is *not* the centerfold of *Playboy* magazine. Every roll of fat, every wrinkle, every wart, every blemish—that's what the artist draws. What you see is what you get. You thought no one knew about that double chin when you are looking down! They will draw that first. There are no soft lights, nor artfully draped fig leaves, wreaths of mist, or strategically placed flowers and ferns to conceal those private parts. *All* is revealed.

You have to grow accustomed to people squinting at you from behind their easels (I've had it explained to me, the squinting, but I couldn't explain it to you) or holding a pencil at eye level, then closing one eye while the other solemnly surveys your nude body (I don't know why they do that either). You are an object d'art and will be discussed as such: "Jim, see that left buttock? Get it with charcoal no. 3 and then shade it in no. 5, OK?" "Up from the right breast toward the shoulder, see that shadow?" "I really like that skin tone! Combination of off-yellow and dirty pink!" Unless you are seriously into Lenten penance, or a former Trappist who misses the discipline, never, ever peak behind the easel. The shock may lower your self-esteem to a point beyond therapy: your left buttock is painted green, the right breast is a pomegranate or a cubist abstraction, and your skin tone is far beyond the help of Max Factor. And your hair needs cutting.

All of this leads to the Great Truth that overweight clerics and paunchy prelates of all persuasions would do well to acknowledge: *The body never, ever lies*—especially the naked body. And so to requirement number three: *truth*. Humankind in general may not be able to bear too much reality, but your average art student has no such problem. They are way ahead of seminary students, if this be virtue. Brother Lee Brunner (of blessed memory), an Anglican liturgical dancer, heard a gasp of horror from the congregation when he stepped out in a more-than-adequate loin cloth to perform his Passion piece. The crucifix on the wall above was much less modest—but then that was only a piece of art work. As I pull my dress over my head and arrange myself on the dais, one of my meditations is of all my sisters and brothers—especially in third world countries—who sell their bodies for sex, not art, often to keep from starving. Or else my mind will travel back in time to Jesus stripped naked and mocked, or Bathsheba innocently stepping into her bathtub on that auspicious day when King David lusted after her naked form from the next rooftop. Or Mary during her third trimester, slowly pulling up her dress to admire the marvelous swelling that was the Christ child to come.

However, for all you aspiring models, I believe the overwhelming requirement is number four: *hope*. Modeling is sensual, but not sexual, and as a survivor of incest as a child, I find a sense of reparation and restoration in that quiet, safe sitting. As a child, I always understood that the place where art happened—theater, dance or artist studio—was somehow sacred, and certainly safer, warmer, kinder than most of the church buildings I remember. God always seemed close to me as I leaned, breathless with excitement, over the edge of the last balcony ("the gods") in the theater, or walked, hushed by beauty, into the National Gallery on Trafalgar Square, or heard the orchestra tuning up or the jazz band play. "Yes!" they seemed to say to their Creator—"Oh yes yes yes!" I do believe in the resurrection of the body and life everlasting, but this has absolutely nothing to do with any speculation on life after death. I am *much* more interested in life after birth—and any nonsense about some point in the future (whatever that means) when the body "incorruptible" will be brought from the grave (preferably at age twenty-three, when I had the most fabulous suntan ever) is hubris, not hope. "In my flesh I shall see God"—that has happened already. It has happened as incest victims have claimed the damaged Temple as theirs alone, and infinitely beautiful; as a sixty-five-year-old uncle who had not swum in fifty years plunged into the ocean and emerged joyous, delighted with his wonderful and still-swimming body; in the everyday miracle of watching a toddler learn to walk or a squirrel fly from a tree, all of these are as miraculous as a portrait by Ingres or Botticelli.

This is true hope—that, through grace, we can look upwards and forwards in spite of rape, incest, cancer, AIDS, gunshot wounds, birthmarks, Grandpa's flat feet, and Grandma's big thighs. Like the artist, we pronounce *all* that God has made *very good*.

The model is a tiny part of this creative process, but when I am sitting starkas, in my birthday suit (*why* so many euphemisms?) staring at the stained glass windows (two of the art centers where I model are former churches), I can almost feel that life pulse. Sometimes I wonder if Jesus would not feel more at home here than in the very sanitized, overdressed, sometimes sterile atmosphere of the "real" churches next door.

One day, a visitor from out of town opened the wrong church door and discovered me sitting there naked. The poor fellow almost died of horror, and rushed next door to his meeting, complaining bitterly—as ashamed as Adam. It is sad to think that if he is celibate, that may have been his only glimpse of a fellow creature as God made her.

If sex offenders in prison and treatment centers were made to confront the naked adult body with all its power—from the point of view of the artist (under very strict supervision, to be sure), would that not heal as much as all those hours of expensive talk therapy? Expressive therapists tell stories of the resurrected bodies of men and women who were raped or tortured, who finally learn to love themselves again; and maybe that is what the Creed is talking about. That kind of faith and hope, that kind of bodily resurrection.

The northeastern U.S., where I live, is a cold climate; we are used to bundling up, not stripping down. Our inheritance includes the Puritans and many prissy Protestants and Catholics who, like Tartuffe, often cry "cover your shame!" I understand that modeling is not everyone's way of earning $10 an hour. But those same teenaged daughters who are so appalled at Mom's modeling will parade across the beach in bikinis that are scarcely more concealing than nakedness. I would not feel comfortable on a topless beach, yet if going naked was an integral and important part of the play, I would do it without a qualm. The difference?

I feel supported by the Holy Spirit at the art center. It is my true self sitting there, just as I am without one please. If Jesus or Mary walked into an art class, I think they would take up a brush and start painting. The Gospels tell us Jesus did draw in the sand when the woman taken in adultery was brought to him. Some say he was buying time while he thought up that terrific reply: "Let the one who is without sin cast the first stone." But I think she was an interesting looking lady, so he started to draw her. He never wrote down anything else that we know of (all the epistle-writing was left to Paul), but if his art work was anything like his dramatic ability with stories and language, he must have been terrific.

Air

"The wind bloweth where it listeth, so are all those born of the Spirit."—Jesus

Toads do not fly, so you may feel like delaying some of this until the dove stage. However, for some people, the need to "blow it off" may be necessary right now. As toads sing—and that is a breath-related activity—maybe this is the time for a serious look at air-related problems like chronic asthma, palpitations, fear of suffocation, vertigo, stuttering, stammering, and many other phobias and paralyses. Did the roots of the problem begin in childhood with the abuse? Now is a good time to ask the question.

The foremost signal for the toad to hop out of the pond seems to be talking about "it." There is a beginning stage in the life of the celebrant when suddenly they feel freed up to tell their story—and *everyone* needs to hear about it! I remember this stage very well in my own healing journey. I gave interviews to magazines and told almost any gathering (regardless of need or trust!) about "it." Every time I told my story, it became a little easier; it made the reality (yes, "it" did happen) a little clearer. What was once in the back of the unconscious was now out in the open, aired for all to see—like a filthy old mattress that has been lying in the basement for years and now it is sitting out on the sidewalk, waiting for the garbage truck to come by and dispose of it. Do we really *need* to call out all our friends and neighbors for a viewing? Maybe—until the basement is completely cleaned out. I was helped beyond this "See-Me" attitude by the Zechariahs and Elizabeths of my life, who had seen and heard it all before. The basement of the mind that had formerly seemed so cluttered, so devastating, suddenly became clearer. Missionary zeal and the toad-like sticky tongue that darts back and forth are all part of the scene. The angel Gabriel is quite firm with Zechariah and silences him for nine months, and there are occasions in the healing stories of the Gospels when Jesus tells a person to keep quiet, to wait. Great patience is needed now, and true listening. If you have ever befriended someone with a stammering problem, you will know how necessary it is to provide kind and respectful listening. After an illness or natural circumstance, our toads will become silent for us without our doing anything. What will quiet them? Bronchitis, an accident, a blizzard, a traffic jam, a change of leadership that means you stay put, a pregnancy, a death—all of these phenomena will put the pain of the past into perspective. After all the angry denouncements of John the Baptist, Herod answers his humble prayer, "I must decrease, the Christ must increase," by shutting John up in prison.

In Chapter 11 of St. Luke's Gospel—where we are told, "He was casting out a demon that was dumb"—Jesus himself has a great deal to say: "No sign shall be given this generation except the sign of Jonah…no one after lighting a lamp puts it in the cellar…woe to you lawyers! You have taken away the key to knowledge; you did not enter yourselves and you hindered those who were entering…"

We, celebrants and zambuk together, have opened a door

which cannot now be closed. In the famous picture of Christ knocking on the door of our hearts, there is no handle on his side. We may feel that we need Jesus to break down the door with an iron bar and pull us inside, but the wisdom of the little toad tells us to wait, to lighten up, not to pout (like Jonah), not to argue (like lawyers)—perhaps to try simple, airy, little spells like:

• Blow it off. Take a child's bubbles and let "it" go—with each breath that you take.

• Fly a kite. Make a tail out of all the nasty notes you ever wrote or received: denials of all kinds, from perpetrators, bank managers, insurance companies, employers, bishops, etc.

• Go out in the country at night and look up at the stars and the moon and get in touch with the ancient knowledge that is in astronomy and the phases of the moon, or visit a planetarium.

• Try time-honored ordinary rituals like hanging out the wash on the line on a nice breezy day or working it all through by fixing the car yourself until at last you find out what was making that worrisome noise.

• Do something recitative (those fill-in conversations in opera between the arias). The modern equivalent are rap songs. Chanting, singing, and all music making are healing acts, and child sexual abuse, like other forms of oppression, needs its "We shall overcome someday" songs. Leafing through hymn books, one senses that many were written during the awakening-to-joy-in-the-midst-of-pain period.

• Attend vigils at your local monastery or convent. Getting up *purposely* at 3:30 a.m., or 5:00 or 6:00, and praying with Trappists, Carmelites, or other contemplatives might be a gift of the Holy Spirit who comes in the "still small voice" of silence.

• If you are an "air head," then your consolation may come from reading and thinking it all through. Is this a good time for research? When the toad is frightened, he ducks his head—many of us ducked our heads into books as a child, and some of us (not me) maintained straight A's at school and gold stars at church. *Choosing* to do this for the right reason may lead down fertile paths. You may even write a book about yourself someday!

Fire

"Why not be turned into fire?"—An Early Desert Father

If earthy people often feel "crumbly" and air people often feel "dissipated," then the fragmentation of "fire people" is that we feel like dry sticks ready to be burned. Is this a "consummation devoutly to be wished for"? I believe so.

I am closest to this element, and those of us who are still working through the residue of our rage will keep returning to this kind of element. As I look back on the history of my own anger, I see a girl, a woman constantly in search of a hearth—a safe container. As a young theater director in Canada, I did a mime play with twenty teenagers on the legend of Prometheus, the Greek god who stole fire and brought it to the ordinary people. I was, and still am, amazingly attracted to this idea. Prometheus was the subject of Beethoven's only ballet music, and he wrote it as he was going deaf (Opus 54). Had he accepted the inevitable? Did he write it out of the fire—the longing of his own soul?

Little toad, held in the hand, what can you teach us about energy and warmth? And the dangers of burn-out and stress?

Looking deeply into a fire or even meditating with a candle, we see how marvelously varied and infinitely different is our creation—a flame that is never the same shape or size for more than a moment. Like the toad, we creatures too can shed our skins, change, and be made new—and we too may have to "eat the old discarded past, digest it" into our innermost selves. The earthy and airy souls can more readily put "it" out there, but fire people need to be very careful. We can so easily become fire that is out of hand. You sense that poor Sonya in *Uncle Vanya* is just worn out from too many little tasks. Women are particularly prone to this. Says Toni Morrison, "We are traditionally rather proud of ourselves for having slipped creative work in there between the domestic chores and obligations. I'm not sure we deserve such big A-pluses for all that." Nor am I, but is there any other way? Do we just sigh, and throw another log on the fire, and carry on regardless in this frantic fashion? Out of its own body, the toad creates a whole new skin. Isn't that remarkable? How does she do it? It cannot be achieved while we are jumping all over the place. And remember, a toad is *not* a frog! Jesus said, "No one puts new wine into old skins; if he does, the new wine will burst the skins and it will be spilled, and the skins will be destroyed" (Luke 5:37-38). Alcoholics Anonymous has provided a "hearth" for those who need a new skin, a container for the fire-water that is killing them.

For me, my art form, acting, has been the new skin that I manufacture out of my temple-self every time I perform. For the actor, the body is *the* instrument in a way that is not true for musicians or artists. The actor is constantly changing skins, and this is a fine and exciting thing to do if the body underneath is able to sustain it all. This was my way of survival as a child: playing the wicked witch or the ugly sisters, I could vent all my anger within the sacred space of the stage. Trusting my intuition to know when to change skins has been my saving grace and the spiritual source of my acting, on stage and off.

In this place I can love and appreciate myself, "celebrate and sing myself" as Walt Whitman puts it. How to get in touch with this energizing fire? I believe the second birthing story in St. Luke's Gospel will give us some clues: "In the sixth month [there is a precision about the timing of *when* Elizabeth is ready to greet Mary] the angel Gabriel was sent from God to a town of Galilee, named Nazareth, to a virgin..." "Virgin!" your victim cries, "I lost my virginity at the age of seven and no angel Gabriel came to rescue me!"

Says John Shea: "We need to be reminded that every second of our survival does really mean that we are new from God's fingers, so that it requires no more than the miracle which we never notice, to restore to us our virgin-heart at any moment we choose." And Mary did choose. So can we. We don't even have to fetch the matches, for God is standing right by, paper lit and ready. We are so afraid. Eft memories of the great value the church has placed on false virginity (the mere physically intact, unviolated vagina), over and above spiritual virginity, can make us retreat from the fire in haste.

The role of the zambuk here is very similar to the role of the angel Gabriel with Mary.

I said to a woman who had been gang-raped as a child: "Maybe Mary was raped too—a young girl in occupied territory, surrounded by foreign soldiers. Would that have made any difference to the Holy Spirit?" "Oh!" she cried, "How wonderful!" And her eyes lit up just as Mary's must have done two-thousand years ago, when Gabriel told her that she was not alone in her strange pregnancy: "For your kinswoman, Elizabeth, whom everyone considered barren, is now in her sixth month. With God all things are possible."

It is difficult for men, particularly celibate men, to understand what the doctrine of the virgin birth has done for the millions of women over the centuries who have had their virginity snatched from them in harmful ways like rape and incest. Unlike Mary, they had no choice. If you are a man counseling a woman who seems fired up over her abuse, please lay aside all your own expectations and listen with your whole self. You may have to accept her angry projections, without judging, and without preconceived ideas.

Male survivors—passionate souls—how can we find the celebrant John of the Cross or Martin Luther King? I am a woman trying hard to be inclusive in my writing, so it is important for me to listen carefully to my fellow male celebrants and to try to identify with the dilemma of Joseph when he learns from that same angel Gabriel that his betrothed virgin is pregnant. Joseph does not immediately leap into action. In effect, he says he will sleep on it, and he pays attention to his dreams. The course of Christian history would have been quite different if Joseph had not been so intuitive. I think he is an excellent role model for survivors and zambuks alike. This may be a good time to write down all your dreams and see what messages they have for you.

There are bound to be surprises. In a dream I had last week, I realized, on waking, that I had given myself permission to heal and to grow throughout the dream sequences.

Who would have thought that the old red curtain at the top of the stairs that I stared at during the abuse could become the rich wine-red velvet of the theater? Or the carpenter from Nazareth would end up in Egypt?

The best of spells for intuitive, fiery souls may be the old-est—like theater, dance, movies. As I was writing this chapter, my insomnia demon was effaced by the memories of seeing the film *Fried Green Tomatoes.* The journey of actress Jessica Tandy back into the past of a feisty, young woman and her friend, warmed my heart at 3:00 a.m. and gave me hope. The overly dra-matic woman who barges into the sedate dinner party at the house of Simon the Pharisee and anoints Jesus's feet, is soothed by the story he tells, as much as anyone else (Luke 7:30-50).

So, go to the movies and the theater, read your way through all of Susan Howatch's dramatic novels on the spiritual life (*Glittering Images, Glamorous Powers, Scandalous Risks, Ultimate Prizes*—and I can't wait for the next one to come out!), and dance!

It is a sad part of modern American life that most people don't dance, over and above the occasional wedding or aerobics class. Men, in particular, once they reach the age of thirty, rarely dance. I envy Native Americans and Africans who can drum and dance the night away, knowing that all that energy is well spent. We are horribly passive, moving from desk to TV set, to car, to computer, to bed, like zombies. No wonder we cannot digest the skins we shed in natural ways! Our churches frown on liturgical dance as "unseemly." When I look back on my adventure-loving dad, who loved to dance and act and sing, I see how frustrated and imprisoned he must have felt by the post-war life as a shopkeeper. Pictures of him taken in the 1950s reveal a paunchy man, dulled by petty business and bored to death—thirsting for adventure, for the *dance*. Back in the 1920s and 1930s, he had been a debonair and daring young soldier—and so handsome.

Toads push with their feet when they are frightened. The desire to push is very strong within me. I wanted to kick away my dad when I was straddled around his neck for oral sex as a child, staring at that red curtain. When I was eight years old, I had chicken pox—and the spots were very much "down there." I heard French cancan music from the radio downstairs, and, picking up my night dress, I pretended I was a cancan dancer. My mother came in and told me "not to be so rude," but I remember that the dancing cooled more than my itching chicken pox.

In some places, like Seattle, dance and movement therapy centers are helping survivors to get in touch with the bodily pain—and so heal. My friend Betsy Beckman has helped hundreds of people towards recovery through dance. It is not just the energy expended, nor the rhythms recalled, but the discipline involved in dance. Many survivors may have problems with steps (twice to the right, four to the left) and with following a partner, but expressive dance, in a free atmosphere, where the process is honored over and above the product, can help us to push away the fear and grow in love toward ourselves.

Water

"The water that I shall give will become to her (or him) a spring of water welling up to eternal life."—Jesus

A novice in a Trappist monastery wrote:

"As teachers and students move through terms or semesters, farmers through the times of planting, growing, and harvesting, I move through the liturgical year. My new life ebbs and flows according to the liturgy and my soul seems to swim in circles within circles, along curves inside cycloids, wrapped around even greater loops, my path segueing effortlessly from one phase to the next. Imagine my life as a tapestry coming off a loom in which small clusters of knots represent a day in my life, each one a flower of color, the smallest discernible element of the tapestry pattern."

This is a beautiful description of the excitement, the joy, of the novice—the celebrant to be. Water rituals remind us of the original safe place within the mother's womb—the home we all long to return to.

I could tell you many tales of how I have been healed by the Hudson River, or the ocean, or just soaking in a good warm tub after a strenuous day. But I think fellow celebrant Sister Peg Widman, R.S.M., in her poem to Mother God, describes the metamorphosis so beautifully. She is led, like the psalmist, to "still water" and so can reflect back to where all was well, and forward to where all shall be well. Like the toad, she has absorbed healing waters into herself—and so she can change and heal accordingly.

MOTHER GOD

I open my eyes
fearful
alone
and slowly I feel her
Warm skin
Different on the outside
Than from the inside
Slowly I realize I am
Wrapped in her arms
As surely as I was
wrapped in her womb
She is looking at me
She has been looking at me
For a long time
Waiting for me to open my eyes

A past of pain and fear
Blurs my vision
What if she too is a stranger?

Her gaze is steady
Waiting
And when I finally look

I see myself
And she sees herself
In the eyes of Mother God I see myself reflected
And know that Mother God sees herself reflected in my eyes
The spark of recognition
Lights us both with laughter
Her breast is waiting
Full
I am astonished
A God so caring for me
The spark of recognition in our eyes
Gives me courage to trust such loving
I suddenly miss the taut cord
Empty
Bewildered
I do not know what to do
With her breast
Her fingers gently caress my
Cheek and soon I am grasping
The tightness
And lean into the warmth of soft skin
I feel her running life filling the emptiness of fear with peace
I stop to look again
Her eyes still mirror me

—Sister Peg Widman

Baptism is the great public ritual of cleansing. A private christening ceremony may also announce the new birth. For Sister Peg, whose abuser was her mother, coming to know Mother God through the experience of a retreat that culminated in the writing of this poem was water metamorphosis. We are no longer "stuck in the birth canal of God," but bathed in God's loving care. There are many biblical stories that attest to this power: the dangers of drowning in the Red Sea or being stuck for years by the pool of Bethsaida, like that whining idiot who does not want to be healed (John 5:1-15-18)! God only knows why Jesus picked *him* out of all the sick ones lying around! Maybe Jesus saw that he was at the toad stage and he didn't even know it himself?

These water rituals have more to do with the refreshment of the emerging grown-up toad than with the weeping of the previous chapter. In the private encounter at night between Jesus and Nicodemus (John 3:1-17), changes are beginning in the spiritual water of the womb, which will culminate in Nicodemus's decision to throw in his lot with Jesus and assist Joseph of Arimathea in the burial of Christ (John 19:39).

Says another celebrant sister:

AUGUST

I never expected the bottom line to be birth.
Entered, the heart of the maelstrom
Re-done, primitive history.
It is time—a world
(light-point small from womb perspective)
waits.

But oh! to trust
these fluid-bound lungs to pump speech for me,
this throat to name my name.
Light, air—so longed for
surprise skin
shock the eyes and lungs.
I yield to deepening contractions
agony
of necessary separation.

You
coach breath
heed cries of pain and wonder
steady my emerging self with midwife's hands
and heart.

A start of recognition.
I can look into your eyes
now that we have separate faces
separate forms
solid ground between us.

Whatever happens, this is.
Forever
the careful, treasured knot
at my center—
sturdy cord of a self
lent
until a second self is sure.

In 1962, an eleven-year-old girl became pregnant. Without ever saying anything to her directly, her grandmother took her to the "doctor." The "doctor's" office was in a very seedy part of a strange city, the pain was harrowing, the girl bled for weeks, and she had no idea until much, much later what was happening to her. Nor will she ever know if she was impregnated by her father, or by the stranger who had raped her that spring.

The girl had already developed a multiple personality disorder as a way to protect herself from the terrors of her young life, but neither she nor anyone else knew what was really going on in her psyche until thirty years later. But then just last month, after "waking up" from a period of several days during which she had left her own consciousness because of the pain she was in and several of her "alters" had taken care of her, she had the following dream:

> *She was in a clearing in a very ancient and very beautiful forest. There were many other creatures there: several adult women quite like herself, young girls, a young boy, adolescent girls, a teen-age boy, an old woman, several ani-*

mals, mythological characters, abstract con-
cepts somehow personified. She knew some of
them much better than others, but somehow
knew all of them and knew them to be friendly.
They welcomed her with their smiles.

Then she turned toward the other side of the
clearing and saw many fearsome creatures—the
Red Hats, Banshee, Aawry, Grindost, all of
whom she knew somewhat—but also other loath-
some, foul-smelling, demonic creatures, crea-
tures she could not bear to face, and she was
overcome by terror. But then the most loathsome,
foul, fearsome creature of all spoke to her and
said: "You need not fear us, if you but love us."

The scene shifted, and she was in an open
place, and was completely enveloped by a vast
radiant cloud. And she was overcome by longing
and grief and cried out to the cloud in agony:
"But why did you cast me away from thy pres-
ence, and take thy Holy Spirit from me?" And
then all that vast universe of radiance coalesced
and became a person. And he knelt by her bed
and took her face in his beautiful, wounded
hands and wiped all the tears from her eyes. And
he spoke to her and said: "Frances, I know all of
you, and I love all of you. I will always be with
you, and the darkness will not overcome you.
Just let me love you."

Frances arranged for a service in her local parish, to which
close friends and family were invited, to—in her words—"have a
time of mourning for the child who could not be born, ask for
healing for those who survived, and, in the Holy Eucharist, celebrate the new life that is given to us so abundantly." This was followed by a house blessing and party at her home. It was a very
healing ritual for Frances and for those who had walked with her

on parts of her journey. Telling her transformative dream publicly (it was printed both on her invitations and in the service leaflet) was a wonderful way to make her experience of metamorphosis (and ours) more "real" by sharing it with her community. Her story is not finished yet, but those of us who participated in the service were blessed to be included in part of it.

—————

"There once was a man who had two sons…"

These are magic words. Through hearing of another's plight, we are somehow less vulnerable, less lonely in this difficult world. The storyteller, by using his or her imagination, helps us to escape from a reality that is often too painful to deal with. With this freedom, we come to know that we are loved just as we are—and so we are healed and can move forward in faith. Storytelling comes to the problem of being human in a world of sin and suffering from the sidelines, indirectly, not competitively, refusing to argue or debate an issue. Stories persuade and cajole us.

In poor countries, storytelling is often a fine art. I imagine it as much as it was in Jesus's time. The greater the oppression, the greater the need for story—either to divert the attention from the pangs of hunger or pain or to pass the idle hours while you are unemployed, or as relief from backbreaking work, such as picking cotton or grapes. (I am sure slaves had more stories to share and greater skills in the art than slave owners!) Stories also amuse the children who really should be in school. Word spreads around the village like wildfire: "The storyteller is here!" And the people gather in the place, or the piazza, or the plaza, or the house in Capernaum, and listen! How did Jesus attract their attention, these famous tax gatherers and "sinners" who usually made up the audience? The Pharisees or Scribes were more interested in systematic theology and debate than little tales of mustard seeds and lost coins. Perhaps a large percentage of Jesus' audience were women and children, who later grew up and remembered the stories and repeated them to the Gospel writers.

The parables fulfilled a need not only for the listeners but also for the storyteller himself. Take the story that occurs in the midst of that embarrassing situation at the house of Simon, the Pharisee. The scene is set: Jesus is already feeling needy, for "no one kissed him when he entered or gave him any water for his feet." At his head are all these suspicious Pharisees, and at his feet this weeping woman with all the perfume and hair. Jesus is trapped in the middle between head and heart, male disapproval and female emotionality, a right brain-left brain dilemma if ever there was one—not to mention the effect on his own body (foot kissing can be very erotic!). It's a potentially dangerous situation, especially for Jesus. So he tells a story and the situation is put into a whole new perspective of love and forgiveness, and balance and wholeness are restored to all.

hold me fast
don't let me pass

VII THE EEL:

THE "F"
WORD–
FORGIVENESS

The transition from the world of the little toad to the extraordinary eel is as individual as the infinite varieties of fish that I viewed all day yesterday with my cousin Jake at the New York aquarium at Coney Island. It was a cold February Monday. I had spent the previous weekend at a retreat house, with a dozen or so women and three monks who cared for us all with touching tenderness. As I looked out over the gray, wintry Atlantic Ocean at Coney Island, I remembered the warmth as we gathered around a blazing log fire on Saturday night. Even more endearing was the remembrance at Sunday dinner of a monk with a picnic basket, setting off to the hermitage for a hurt woman and her kind zambuk who needed to finish out some healing business in private. It is of such that the kingdom of heaven is made—such carefulness can turn the rituals of the toad into "a sea-change," as Shakespeare describes it in Ariel's song in *The Tempest*. In that play, also, Prospero says, "Now I want Spirits to enforce; art to enchant and my ending is despair unless I be relieved by prayer which pierces so that it assaults Mercy itself and frees all faults."

Above all else, we cannot climb Calvary without Gethsemani. The only creature that cannot survive in Janet's arms is the eel. A fish needs water. I think the "letter from a novice" (in the previous chapter) highlights an important element in the healing journey that I glimpsed through the glass of the aquarium: a contemplative view of time. We are talking now of eels, not sharks or porpoises that swim endlessly and never rest. The rhythm of the eel is that of repose and undulating movements—often in one corner of the fish tank. What can this strange, snake-like, watery fish have to tell us about our life in Christ as celebrant? Can the adder that symbolized the toxic shame and guilt of abuse become the eel, a very different kind of snake? I asked the eels and they spoke to me of a world that is as time-less and effortless as a beautiful ballet, or a Bach fugue exquisitely played, or a life lived in total acceptance of the here and now—of what is.

From an encyclopedia entry for eel:

> Naturalists have found the unusual life history and reproductive habits of the eel very interesting. Both European and American eels have their breeding grounds around the Bermuda Islands. They swim out from the fresh water streams into the ocean only at spawning time when they are ready to lay their eggs. This comes in the fall. The parent eels die after they have spawned. The young appear sometime during the following spring. When small, they are so thin and transparent that the print on this page could be read through their bodies. Young American eels appear in fresh-water streams the second spring, when they are a year old. They

are then about three inches long. The European species do not appear in rivers until they are three years old. Young eels that are migrating upstream are called elvers. Females go far inland, but the males remain in tidal waters. Eels are caught for market as they are migrating downstream to lay their eggs in the sea. They are taken in nets, by hand and set lines, and in small wire traps called eel pots. They can also be speared while lying in the mud. Their flesh has an excellent taste and makes good food.

The eel follows an unusual pattern, dying that others may live. It is this kind of "dying" that must be done right now—the moment of Jairus's daughter, Mary and Martha's brother, and all of our daughters and brothers. It is the new birth that Jesus speaks of with Nicodemus in that nighttime encounter over the flickering lamp. It is the raging thirst of the Samaritan woman at the well. Suddenly assuaged, she "dies" to her old life and takes up the new. It is Jesus dying with us, birthing us—Jesus our mother shedding blood and water. Do all of us, in our deep, deep unconscious, not recall the blood and the water that enfolded us at birth? Sister Peg's poem speaks so eloquently of the God who "mirrors" us. We may be as tiny and transparent as a newborn eel, but there is new life. It is unsuspected, a surprise, but very real.

As with the eels, there may be a pattern in our silence and solitude, our pain and delivery, that is gender-related. Some females may *not* "go far inland," and some males *may* penetrate beyond the tidal waters, but neither is the norm. I am no Jungian psychologist, no expert, and I am dealing with a very slippery subject. Do we need to put on gloves to handle our eels? I think not. Janet just held on to her eel for dear life—knowing that it was but a process in Tam Lin's transformation. We can, all of us, do worse.

Now is a time for silence that is quite different from the imposed silence of the earlier stages of the adder. "Silence" may be a dirty word to many survivors, when there was no choice but to obey the abuser and keep quiet. Many placards, signs, and books proclaim "Silent No More!" Is it possible to reconcile the "bad silence" of the adder with the "good silence" of the eel? The pseudo-Pauline edict is that women must remain silent in church. One of the things women have kept silent about is incest. We have had no voice in the ruling bodies of society. Is it any wonder that as women gain a broader voice in government, we should begin to speak of the unspeakable? It is hard for us to articulate the female silence of the 3:00 a.m., ninth-month-of-pregnancy-watch, or the breast-feeding in the early dawn. Women have always known that if we had accompanied Jesus to the Garden of Gethsemani, we would have had no trouble staying awake! We are used to it!

How is the silence and solitude of women different from that of men? Maybe the time has come for church*men* to lay aside for a while the works of Thomas Aquinas and Augustine, Thomas Merton and Dietrich Bonhoeffer and listen to the lives of women who are the great black writers of our day, such as Toni Morrison and Alice Walker. Or read the novels of Virginia Woolf and the sermons of women priests. Give a forum to those women and girls who have gone "far inward," in the spirit of, maybe because of, intense suffering. It is true we have not written of it very much—and why is this? We were just too busy, too tired, or we died too young. We had no money, no time, and no education. For many of us, the desert silence is not *chosen,* as it was in the case of many male prophets, like John the Baptist, but enforced, as it was for Hagar. Many women have had to "become male" in order to move into the outer limits. I think the eel can teach us something here. I would like to invite the men to imitate the female eel and go swimming in the far inland waters of deep maternal silence—the unknown territory of the pregnant one, knowing that this trip is not for yourself but for the new life to come. I would invite you to enter into a solitude and poverty of spirit not born of the luxury of *choice.* Jesus sought out silence and solitude only *after* eating with hoards of people, prostitutes, tax gatherers—the whole mess of humanity. He often seemed to seek protection by getting into a boat, much as a mother does when she goes to the bathroom for a little privacy (and still the little ones come knocking at the door!).

What can women learn from the male eels resting in the caves of the ocean, slithering through the tidal water at the mouth of the river, waiting for the return of the females and for death? The single-mindedness of a man like St. Anthony, who left his family and went into the desert, or like Shakespeare, who left his wife and children in Stratford and went into the swirling waters of the Elizabethan London theater scene, there to act and write beside the river Thames. Jesus tells us—younger sisters, brothers, mothers waiting outside the door, entreating him to come home with us to safety and protection—that we must do the word of God in the vast tidal oceans of humanity and that this will entail laying down our life in order to take it up again. The problem for many women, both victims and zambuks, is that we have no life to lay down in the first place—we are only the sum total of what others expect us to be. I have encountered several multiple personality disorder survivors, and there are so many "selves" and yet no True Self. Can we throw a woman or a man like that into the mainstream of life? An enormous task of re-parenting needs to be done—not only with very fragile souls, but with all of us who have allowed ourselves to be named and known by the roles we played or the fact that we were born female or male.

In the Gospels, someone calls out to Jesus: "Blessed is the womb that bore you and the breasts that gave you suckle!" But Jesus, in effect, negates both of those female aspects of womanhood and says, "No. Blessed is she who hears the word of God and does it!" It is a blessed thing to explore these tidal reaches of ourselves unencumbered by the importance of breasts and wombs. Perhaps this is why so many women come to new life after menopause. I speak as a woman of fifty who hasn't touched a box of Tampax in months and handed over the last bottle of Midol (painkillers for menstrual cramps) to a daughter. We can rebirth our true virginity in this time of trial. Remember that if Mary had been a young wife and mother, she would not have had the freedom to stand at the foot of the cross where she was need-ed. She would have been with the "daughters of Jerusalem," those women who stood at the distance. We can get closer to the cross when we are free from other responsibilities.

At this stage in the journey, we are no longer the adolescent with the red-hot iron rage. We have been through the "twenties" of the toad; we now approach the beginning of mid-life in a "dying" that allows God's mercy and forgiveness to flow. Jesus was thirty-three when he died on the cross, and those days that was probably the peak of maturity. In the twentieth century, we have extended adolescence way beyond puberty, well into the twenties, with college and postponed marriages, so we may not be equipped to "set our face toward Jerusalem" until we are in our forties or fifties.

The author's father, about thirty years old, fishing in India.

Who were his pro-cele-brants, his zambuks, as he faced Holy Week? A motley crew indeed, and often it was the unexpected ones who proved the love and care and concern that facilitated the forgiveness.

This forgiveness should not be confused with reconciliation. It is more like giving away the pain to the only one who can truly heal: God. My dad never ever said he was sorry for what he had done to me as a child. I have never heard of a perpetrator falling down on his/her knees and begging forgiveness—*unless* there has been a real "crucifixion," like a long prison sentence. It is more a question of letting go of the past, not letting your life be ruled by the incest.

The closest my dad ever came to asking for my forgiveness was after his first cancer operation when he, like me, was plagued with insomnia. I asked him what he thought about during those long, difficult nights. "Fall to ruminating!" he replied. "On what?" I asked. "Oh, things from the past, your childhood…" "Things between you and me?" "Yes," he answered. I could have picked up the conversation and forced a confession at that point, but suddenly I looked at him not with pity but with mercy. It was like the pus draining away from a very old wound, leaving only clarity, kindness, and emptiness between us.

When, later on, I confronted him about Missy, I set the scene like an actor, making sure that the moment was just right: Dad was sitting down, I was upstage, well-grounded, poised, waiting in the wings. When I came out on stage and uttered these opening lines, Mercy came and stood beside me like a guardian angel. Pity receded backstage, and I let myself become my Truest, Bravest, Best me. I said, "Dad, it was wrong—it was a wicked thing that you did to Missy." I was king of the castle. He was the dirty rascal.

This was something I needed to do alone. Others may need a zambuk with them, "when Mercy seasons Justice." It may be in a courtroom full of people, as it was in Shakespeare's *The Merchant of Venice*.

The ones who journey up Calvary with us will be those who choose to do this, the mature ones like Mary, the beloved disciples, the family, the Magdalene from whom he cast out seven demons.

Coming to this place of pain and torture is the ultimate truth. We can only do it right when it is a choice, freely made, freely accepted, as Jesus did. The difference is that Jesus was wholly innocent and we are not. We ask for forgiveness of our own trespasses, even as, through God's grace alone, we offer forgiveness to the other. We approach the cross…

Now that we are here—close enough to listen—what is it that we see and hear? We see the nakedness of the Innocent Beloved. It makes us feel such an outgoing rush of pity, for we know this body: the hands that once played the first century equivalent of patty-cake, now driven with nails; the knees that still bear the scar where the child fell after being set upon by bullies at the synagogue one Sabbath.

I remember the intimacy of personality that I felt as I gently undressed my dad in the little bathroom of the mobile home that sits amidst the green pastoral Kentish countryside. A woman told me that an enema for her was a form of torture used by her abusive father when she was a child, but for Dad it was a blessed relief. How I admired his courage, and the beauty of his eighty-seven-year-old body—kept lean and lovely through the latter years by exercise, good diet, vacations, and constant catharsis of spirit and mind. "Super chap, your father!" said the Anglican priest, when we laid Dad's ashes to rest in the country churchyard. Through shining eyes, I agreed, "Yes, a super chap." On my dad's gravestone is written: "Gone Fishing." My dad was not just any old fisherman; he was a fly fisherman. Trout was what he loved to fish! He saw trout fishing as a mystical, contemplative experience. Certainly he felt closer to God on a river bank than he did in church. To leave the burdens of everyday dull care and venture out, often all night, frequently in some place that said "no fishing"—this was real living. I remember he risked the wrath of the water bailiff on many occasions to bring us home a delicious speckled trout or a meaty eel. Between the fisherman and his eel—ah, such sport! What bait to use? How do you go bobbing to eels? How can Janet hold fast to something so elusive?

I believe John the Baptist and perhaps Peter the fisherman would hold up the eel as the most important part of the healing journey. A wonderful little story about healing from child abuse and the role of the zambuk is *The All of It* by Jeannette Haien. Set on the west coast of Ireland, it tells of how new life and love are birthed between a dying brother and his sister (both victims of child abuse) and the priest zambuk (who also happens to be a fisherman). Often, as I say the words "forgive us our trespasses, as we forgive those who trespass against us," I smile, because the words bring to mind the numerous "trespassers will be prosecuted" signs that my dad ignored on those wild Sunday afternoon fishing expeditions—when forgiveness began its work.

After the comforting enema, back onto the sofa bed in the living room, Dad confided that when the pain was very bad on some nights, he often felt like "throwing in his fishing rods"—his way of talking about death. Suicide was something that Dad and I learned to reject over and over again, through my mother, but the good self-pity and self-mercy can open us up to the honesty of the words from the cross:

"My God, my God, why hast thou forsaken me?"

The loneliness and alienation are acute, but unlike the powerlessness of the mighty lion, we know enough now to believe there is a God out there who could help us. This God is not the punishing, mean-spirited, bully-god that we often thought was watching us from a distance as children—for we have rejected these lies in earlier healing—but this God is just "God"—not "Abba, Father." "Mine"—yes—but somehow right now, not available. This is what my dad felt when he grappled with cancer during all those months before the benediction of morphine. Mary, watching Jesus, overhearing these words, did you know this couldn't be the "last word?" In St. Mark's Gospel, it is the last recorded saying of Jesus, which perhaps tells us not to make too much of words—for even if Jesus had been entirely silent during his ordeal on the cross, the action of his dying would have been eloquence enough. Words are, in the end, only little transitory things.

It is a terrible honor to be privy to the intense alienation and loneliness of a priestly person working through the suffering with a distant, deaf God, knowing that you can do nothing else but just be there. No use interrupting and saying "I haven't abandoned you!" He or she cannot even see you standing there, because of the tears and the blood and the great surging tidal waves of pain. But hold on to the reality that the question, wrenched from the deep, angry place, is rhetorical. My God, Jesus's God, your God is now silent to the cries of anguish from the little ones, and the only thing we, as a mother or a beloved disciple, can do right now is to do what God, our Mother, God our Beloved, does for us: suffer along. I take my dad's pain, through the agent of pity, into my own being and just let it sit there. It will do no good for us to scream in outrage too, like a mourner at an Irish wake. That time is long past. We must just be there with the pain. As I bent over Dad's body and looked at the member that had caused me so much suffering as a child, I felt a rush of pity for myself as well as for him. Margery Kempe, that memorable medieval sister mystic of Julian, records a similar moment of grace as she tended her naked, dying husband and the father of her fourteen children.

It is such a mixture of feelings: "My" God—intimate and close—but, at this moment, somehow "forsaken." Yet, I sympathized with God then. God seems to say to the sufferer: "This is what you need to do for yourself. I will keep my distance, for in this moment, you must be alone—just yourself—not *my* beloved son, Bob, but everyman, anywhere, birthing death. I am not as distant as I appear to be. Yes, it is the ninth hour and there is darkness all about you, which may make me obscure. But, remember, darkness always turns to light. That is my promise to you." This is the eel gasping for breath outside of its watery home—in Janet's hands, or wherever it is that parent eels go to die after spawning. If you have ever watched a fish writhing on a hook, you will notice a moment of stillness and surrender, as if the body of the eel knows that this is it.

We now come to the "F" word, *forgiveness*. I think that St. Peter, the fisherman, might have placed this word like a prize fish down in the center of all our lives. We do well to ponder that the fish for early Christians was a more central symbol for their new life than the cross—and that "forgiveness" is a favorite word on the lips of Jesus.

"Father, forgive them for they know not what they do."

The distant one now seems to come closer to his/her son, and Jesus can name "Abba, Father" as a source of a new way of being with the pain. Note that Jesus does not claim this forgiveness for himself; it is not "*I* forgive them." To paraphrase what I hear him saying: "Daddy, I don't find it in myself at this moment when I am in such pain to forgive those who have hurt me, but I know from experience that you have the power to do that for me—and I ask you to take on that work for me. My understanding of my abusers surprises even me, but now I've said it out loud and others have heard it, so I'll say it again. They know not what they do. I don't know where this compassion comes from, but you're the Parent of us all, so work this through me as you will." And it happens. Why? Is forgiveness a magic trick, the fairy godmother waving her wand to make it all better? Absolutely *not*. Forgiveness is something that I believe Jesus forged in the everyday living among tiresome disciples and well-meaning mothers and brothers, not to mention all those testy lawyers, picky Pharisees, and sarcastic scribes. And not to mention the forgiveness of self, when the miracle didn't work or when the tax gatherers said, "I don't get it," the first time he told a parable. (So if sheep and shepherds, coins and housewives don't ring a bell, what if I try, "There was once a man who had two sons...."?)

If "silence" is a dirty word for survivors, "forgiveness" is the "F" word *par excellence*! "You want me to forgive that bastard for what he did to me?" "I *will never never never* forgive her!" In writing this book, I feel as if I really want to throw the whole thing out the window and just write about the fathomless depths of forgiveness that have come to me through the little window of my understanding: "They know not what they do." In essence, the whole book is about forgiveness. It is with relief that I realize I don't have to say the last word on forgiveness in this little chapter—or ever. I don't have the last word. I would never dream of prescribing anything for anyone else, but let me briefly tell you what has happened to me in coming to be a *little more gentle* with:

- my Abba—God
- my little girl-self who got hurt
- my grown-up woman-self
- my world, my neighbor (which includes my abused and

abusing church), and the chain of abuse from the whole human family, dragged through the centuries, on every continent.

Forgiveness, for me, has happened throughout my life—as many times as there are eels in the mouth of the River Medway where my dad used to fish. It is not something that I have done myself; it is a gift from my Abba to me. All I have to do is accept it. Forgiveness is the horse; I am the rider. It waited for me, patiently stabled by my house, all these years—and at times, I have been able to gird up my loins and jump on. When this has happened, with great speed and infinite wonder, I have been taken far from home—out of myself. Like the paralyzed man in the Gospels who is let down through the roof, I have heard that my sins are forgiven and I can now get up, take up my bed, and go home. The journey is always home. Jesus tells the Pharisees that this is a very difficult, painful thing to do, especially when we feel paralyzed over so many years. We are all baptized into forgiveness of sins, so the paradox is that it is also very easy, because the Holy Spirit is there, urging us on, giving us a lift upwards and onwards. To turn from horses back to eels, it is also the simple/natural thing

Flowers for the funeral of the author's father, in All Saints Church, Biddenden, Kent.

for the parent eel to do: for this moment, we were born. So the eel dies and the baby begins to emerge.

The first thing that human babies do is to echo Jesus' words from the cross:

"Woman, behold."

This is a generic "woman"—not necessarily "mother"—but

anyone who will help me cut the cord, clear the nostrils for breathing, or provide an environment in which the new life can be made comfortable. It is the "home" to which forgiveness returns. It is the lifegiving waters of the river or ocean for the baby eel. For me, "woman" has been my therapist, Felice, and countless others. They have always turned my face back again toward the door: "Behold your Son!" When we begin to love ourselves, forgive ourselves, we can begin to love our neighbor. This is a gentle thing, for "the quality of mercy is not strained." It is a cyclical healing that flows between Jesus, his mother, and the beloved disciple, rather like the action of the Trinity, or a Celtic cross, where we are all in this together. I've felt it—and so perhaps have you. There was the bonding I felt between an abbot, a monk, and myself when all the pain of abuse was spread out in front of us, quite naked. We didn't really know which roles any of us were playing, and I was over a thousand miles away at the time. Yet I felt the intimacy of the moment. Who is the victim, who the zambuk, who the celebrant? It does not matter now, for, as Julian would say, "we are all one-ed."

"I thirst!"

Giving birth to my third child, in a more enlightened atmosphere than for the other two, I was able to "mirror" Mother God (as in Sister Peg's poem) a little more easily. My son, Paul, was an easier birth and immediately, even in the delivery room, I nursed him. What a darling boy he was, and what a thrill! I have had moments of great ecstasy, breast-feeding in silence and solitude. When I have spoken to other mothers, they tell me the same thing. Ask a nursing mother to try to speak of it to you. First, she will be amazed that anyone should ask about anything so ordinary, and then maybe she will dig around for words, and then maybe you will hear something quite extraordinary. What you hear will tell you about the child's instinctive understanding that he or she has a right to satisfaction in this life. Watch an animal nursing her young or an elderly man, like my dad, sitting up in bed and enjoying a cup of tea—after a night of horror—looking out of the window at the new day.

When I have been able to admit my needs and state them simply and clearly—"I thirst"—there have always been available "the vinegar sponges." Matthew's account of this part of the passion (Matthew 27:47-50) differs from John's, because the bystanders appear to be somewhat confused Jews, who want to know if Elijah will come and work a miracle. John's Gospel states that Jesus knew that all was now finished and so said "I thirst" to fulfill the Scriptures (John 19:28-29). May an actress intervene here in favor of the Matthew account? Very rarely do dying people ever act so self-consciously—as "to fulfill Scripture." They are like newborn babes; "I thirst" is more like the nuzzling of the child at the breast, an instinctive thing.

When my dad died in the early hours of May 8, 1991 (Feast of Dame Julian of Norwich in the Anglican calendar), he did so peacefully, in his sleep—having almost finished off a nice glass of beer. When my youngest brother arrived at the Canterbury hospice, he found that Dad had indeed "Gone Fishing"—and all that remained were the dregs in the bottom of the near-empty glass. When Bruce told me the story over the phone, it seemed a fitting symbol, and it calmed my grief immediately. Dad left me that empty beer glass to remind me to pay attention to my needs, especially those of the body, for we cannot live without water, however it comes. There will be confusion as to how this is to be administered, but ultimately someone will offer the sour wine (or beer). We will drink it down—and John would tell us that it is then all over. That is *his* perspective. Let us take up Luke's story, which sits better with an actress, who knows the importance of fellow actors on stage: the other two men, crucified on either side of Jesus (Luke 23:39-43).

"Truly, I say to you, today you shall be with me in paradise."

Another threesome: two thieves and a third. This time, the play—Dante's *Divine Comedy*—is enacted horizontally, rather than vertically as in the previous scene. All three actors are assigned their stage sets, rather like a medieval mystery play, with Jesus in the middle. No wonder so many painters of that time could bring rich detail and vivid imagination to the image of Christ suffering between two others: one thief who is in a quiet place with his pain and the other in a different, noisier place. I hesitate to put labels on them, such as "the repentant and unrepentant thief." How do we know? (Maybe the one man heard Jesus cry out "My God, my God, why hast thou forsaken me?" and this gave him permission to call out: "Are you not the Christ? Save yourself and us." I know *exactly* how he feels.)

Jesus' promise to the man who recognized Jesus' goodness and his own wrongdoing is the same promise he makes to all of us: paradise. *All* speculation—on sinfulness, pain, and suffering—is merely speculation. I don't know whether Dad is in "heaven" or "hell," but I do know that Jesus promised him (and me) paradise. All the judgment belongs to the Lord of paradise, and he is the one who speaks of hope. Not that all *is* well—but *shall* be—even in the midst of pain and dying. The last time I saw Dad alive was the fourth Sunday of Advent, 1990, when the chaplain at the hospice gathered those who were able, in wheelchairs and beds, for the morning service. "He won't make it to Christmas," the nurse had told me when I arrived in Canterbury. (He lasted till the following May, returning home from the hospice on January 1 to work on a little unfinished business, even do a little fishing!) I cried all the way through the Advent service when Dad sang "All Things Bright and Beautiful" very loudly and recited the twenty-third Psalm with alacrity. I think I had a peek into paradise. A lovely woman in the next wheelchair, with the kind of soft Kent cockney voice that I grew up with, patted my hand throughout the service, saying, "There! There! Duckie, don't take on so!" The next day, Christmas Eve, as I flew home to my family in America, she died—and what jokes the two of them must be having in paradise! If the two thieves are fellow-sufferers with Jesus, then it is not for the zambuks standing by the cross to utter a word. Those who are dying know things—paradise things—that those at the foot of the cross cannot know.

Luke tells us: "It was now about the sixth hour and there was darkness over the whole land until the ninth hour, while the sun's light failed; and the curtain of the temple was torn in two. Then Jesus, crying with a loud voice, said:

"Father, into thy hands I commit my spirit."

This is what the prodigal son said when he returned home and the father kissed him tenderly, wrapped him in the best robe, and placed a ring on his hand and shoes on his feet. The son dropped the last line of his confessional speech, planned in the pig pen, far away—"Treat me therefore like one of the servants"—and realized that was not necessary. All he said was, "Father, I have sinned against God and against you. I am not fit to be called your son." In the story, the father says *absolutely nothing* to the son. He just lavishes him with love and acceptance. I doubt if he even heard his son's speech! He's already picking out the best robe, the ring, and slippers—and mentally taking the fatted calf out of the freezer. When we accept forgiveness, towards ourselves or others, God always goes wild with delight and starts dancing and making music. Forgiving Dad was one thing, forgiving Mum another, forgiving all Episcopalians yet another, forgiving the entire Catholic Church, including the Protestants, etc., forgiving men, forgiving women—the list is endless. But this prayer speaks of the one thing necessary: forgiving myself! Committing myself to God's hands, and knowing them to be kind and non-abusing, means saying "Abba, Father" in a whole new way. I think my own dad pointed a finger in this direction when I went to him on Saturday, December 22, 1990, and said, truthfully, "Dad, I've got to leave you—got to go home to America for Christmas." "I was just about to say the same thing," he said. "Go, Bobbie, go home. That's where you belong!" Between Dad and me, there was nothing more to be said, anyway.

"It is finished."

Or, maybe "it" had just begun. I could say, the rest was gravy—but we all know that is not true. The eel dies in Janet's arms and is resurrected, not as another eel (that one was eaten and enjoyed with a tasty sauce long ago!), but as the dove, symbol in the church of the Holy Spirit, the Comforter, the Advocate, the Promised One.

It is accomplished. In my show *Masks and Mirrors*, I have a large frame, like a tray, in which are set all the fragments, the symbols, of the Tam Lin story. It is rather like a child's puzzle with the nine different pieces. At any moment, a piece may fall out, but now I recognize it and I know where it goes so I can fit it back in place.

Every time sin enters my life, I can slip back into the old unfinished ways, but now I can pick myself up again and again and again. I remember what it feels like to be forgiven. Jesus had to endure, for my sake, for my dad, for my mom, for my church all the ugliness of the entire Passion story. The rejection, the shame, the blame, the weakness, the denial, the betrayal, the pain. It was bodily; it was psychological; it was spiritual.

Yet the bargain God strikes with me is that if I also take up my cross and follow God's son, there will be an end to it—and the end is beauty and glory. Jesus said in his prayer for his disciples, "Father, the hour has come; glorify your Son so that the Son may glorify you....this is eternal life, that they may know you, the only true God....I glorified you on earth by finishing the work that you gave me to do" (John 17:1-4).

The end was amazing grace.

There is a reason for the entire healing journey: eternity. These are blessed wounds, and the sense of surrender to a death which is also birth is Good Friday.

In *Masks and Mirrors*, I depict Janet's journey to change Tam Lin as a mirror, placed in a frame, made up of large fragments, rather like one of those puzzles for two-year-olds. The frame that holds it all together is for me God—creator, lover, sustainer. In the words of Dame Julian of Norwich, "Our world is a little thing, round like a ball, like a hazelnut, held in God's hands..." So God's hands gently cradle my hazelnut world, and they are the framework in which I wrote this poem back in 1986:

POEM WRITTEN AT A
BREAKTHROUGH POINT

There was a moment, back in January when,
through a glass darkly, I suddenly glimpsed
LIGHT.
And since that breakthrough, I live
with those shattered fragments of
MYSELF.
One by one, I pick them up,
delicately, gently for glass can cut and
HURT.
I examine them carefully—
I take my time for this for me is
NEW.
Now if people ask me, "How are you doing,
ROBERTA?"
I tell them, I am creating new patterns
within the kaleidoscope of my
LIFE.
These are not the old manipulative ways,
the angry dispensation of
JUSTICE.
Rather, I take new cloth to make new garments
trying not to merely patch up the
PAST.
Or, if you will, new skins for new wine,
freshly vinted, clean, celebratory,
AIRY.
Then, having tasted of this, one of these days,
I may come to some
TRUTH.
May yet even taste of the Old,
the mellow vintage, seasoned and
GOOD.

But that's not yet—changing water into wine,
the best in the house, requires
PATIENCE.
My time is not yet come—the lightness
of new wine is still upon
ME.
I sip its fresh raw taste and
glimpse—beyond the shattered glass:
RESURRECTION!

My favorite feast day in the entire church calendar is Ascension Day. It fell on May 9 in 1991, the day after Dad died. The difference between the two "finishes" is not so great for us who know the end of the story as it was for the disciples.

Beyond the pain and suffering and even the glorious wounds is a mystical journey into the Cloud of Unknowing, where we shall know as we have been known. "Lifting up his hands, he blessed them. While he was blessing them, he withdrew from them and was carried up into heaven" (Luke 24:50-51).

This was the primary feeling of that Ascension Day: my dad's life was a blessing and a wounding, and in the cycle of healing I had come to the end of the labyrinth.

Or maybe the beginning?

hold me fast

don't
let me pass

VIII THE DOVE:

PEACE AND THE FREEDOM TO CHOOSE

Where is the zambuk now that the end of the journey is in sight? There is no "closure" necessary, as in therapy, because you have always been in the fabric of my everyday living and will continue to be. What does this allow me to feel? Empowerment, affirmation, friendliness, and perhaps new ways of acting and reacting. The world out there may still be as demanding, as depleting, but I am learning to slow down. The masks of the earlier chapter—my "Runaway Robin" and "Bad Girl"—I am learning very gently to take off. In the days of the red-hot iron and even the toad, I might suddenly tear them off. But now I am learning to be kinder to myself. The wise woman counsels the little girl: be still, in silence, listen! Love yourself as your neighbor!

I told my parish priest that I reexperienced each of the chapters of my book as I was writing and rewriting. The "bad stuff"—the shame, blame, denial, and rage—this raced around in my mind and caused all the old problems like insomnia and stress. The "good stuff," in contrast, is felt in my whole self. Body, mind, and spirit are engaged in peacemaking, boundary setting, trust-making. All of this is girded by prayer—for that is the source of all wisdom and all truth. He asked me what it was like to have all of that inside me. I did not really have an answer for him then, but now I do: It would be difficult and burdensome but for the love of Jesus, who tells me that *his* yoke is easy and *his* burden is light—and this is the reason for the whole journey. Sweetness and joy as the dove takes flight and I am closer to my Tam Lin—my Christ.

I believe the Victorian writer Charles Dickens did more to alert the nineteenth century about the horrors of child abuse than any other single soul. Who, even in our present century, has not known David Copperfield, Oliver Twist, little Nell, or Pip? That Dickens wrote from the remembered pain of his own childhood abuse brings the thought that perhaps the majority of our greatest creative artists have brought forth resurrection from the depths of their own woundedness—maybe as children. Listen to the grown-up Pip in *Great Expectations*, when, like Julian of Norwich, he finds himself in the throes of a near-death experience, a crucifixion:

> That I had a fever and was avoided, that I had lost my reason, that the time seemed interminable, that I confounded impossible existences with my own identity...that I was a steel beam of a vast engine, dashing and swirling over a gulf, and yet that I implored in my own person to have the engine stopped, and my part in it hammered off; that I passed through these phases of disease, I know of my own remembrance. That I sometimes struggled with real people, in

the belief that they were murderers—and that I would all at once comprehend that they meant to do me good, and would then sink exhausted in their arms—I also knew all the time there was an extraordinary tendency in all of these people to settle down into the likeness of Joe.

Brother Joe, a zambuk for the author.

I have been tenderly held in such cherished concern through my own "Joe"—a Trappist monk who has prayed for me throughout these past few months and years. During the writing of these final chapters, I sent him my dad's old robe, the one I remembered from my childhood, to wear like a hair shirt—in reverse—to remind both of us that we are loved and forgiven. This is the true worth of the zambuk as "con-celebrant"—both of us offering the sacrifice of our petty self-condemnation on the altar of our present lives. Likewise, Pip is nursed and resurrected to new life through the tender mercies of the once despised "good parent" of his childhood, the zambuk, Joe Gargery, husband to the abusive "Mrs. Joe," Pip's sister.

Before we leave the world of Charles Dickens, a little tale for the con-celebrant at this post-crucifixion stage—especially if there is a great deal of "weeping for themselves and their children." At Emery House in West Newbury, Massachusetts, where the Anglican monks of St. John the Evangelist hosted a retreat last month, I was touched by the memoirs of an elderly monk: "As a novice was reading out loud at supper of the death of Dora from *David Copperfield*, he dissolved into tears and turned to the prior saying, 'Father, I can't go on with this!' To which the prior, banging on the table, replied, 'Read it, and weep!'"

The author (center), her brothers Bill and Bruce, and her friend (to this day) Jean Rosemary Day, feeding the pigeons in Trafalgar Square, about 1953.

After Good Friday, there will be the lying in period. This may include mourning and weeping, as it did for the disciples and Mary Magdalene (John 20:11-18). Holy Saturday is a feast of hope—spring is coming and the earth receives these "tears" to water the crocuses and snowdrops. We know a peace that comes from the certainty that God, our Creator, will do this for us, disturbing the dark, frozen earth of winter with color and life. Only because we have known the shadow can we claim the light. For if Pip had not "died," he could not have let go of his patterns of childhood abuse. If Julian had not desired a vision (three days and three nights), she would not have enjoyed the glory of her "Revelations of Divine Love." We all have such "Showings." These are mine.

The following poem was written in the winter of 1986. Paul, my son, and I went to visit my parents in England. My last memories of my mother are feeding the pigeons in Trafalgar Square in London. Pigeons are the dove of the common person, living as best as they can in the cities of our world, adorning the pompous statues of stone and bronze, and generally disturbing the peace with their fluttering wings and exciting, erratic, pecking and flying. My mother was very ill at the time and senile in many ways. As with many elderly people, there was great wisdom in the midst of the childlike behavior. My mother was preparing beautifully for death—she was "coneying." This is a medieval word, one that Julian would have known. It means to bury oneself in the ground, like a coney (rabbit). She absolutely refused to wash herself or her clothes. She knew she was dust and to dust she would soon return—so the spilled egg from the spoon held in a shaky hand remained on the favorite old sweater and it was not to be washed off in the name of the little god of hygiene. A message here for the celebrant from my mom is to allow them to be with the wisdom of the dark, rocky, earthy tomb, for theirs are not the ways of the world.

The pigeons in Trafalgar Square knew something that neither my brother nor I, nor any of the bystanders, could fully comprehend: maybe hundreds of birds suddenly arose and flocked around my mother, as if sensing the beauty and mystery of death. The rest of us backed away in fear and awe, but my mother stood her ground and smiled serenely at the wonder of it all, with arms outstretched to feed the birds, like a marvelous child. I have a photograph of that occasion, with one bird sitting right on my mother's head. She seems surrounded by an aura, a halo, and the lovely, soft, grey wings all about her. I remember too, as a child, my mother bringing me up to London in those post-war days for

The author's mother, on the day before she died.

a visit to cousins, or to Westminster Abbey, St. Paul's Cathedral, or a seat in "the gods" at the theater, if we could afford it. The first stop, after leaving Charing Cross Station, was to feed the pigeons in Trafalgar Square. London was all bombed out, the streets full of beggars and wounded soldiers, but the magic of the city was what I remember most—and it was my dear mother who brought me here. Looking back on these last few years of my mother's life, I see the "after-life" she bequeathed to me was the legacy of "letting go" to self-forgiveness and mercy. On her gravestone is written: "Resting Peacefully."

Here is a picture of my mother, taken the day before she died. My older brother Bill arrived at the hospital and wheeled her out into the little Kentish village of Headcorn to enjoy the day with her grandchildren. He bought her a peach from the green grocers and, though she could only smell it and nuzzle it, how lovely to leave life with a peach!

I lay in my parents' bed, looking up at my maternal grandmother's picture on the wall, who in cross stitch had written:

> The Year ahead,
> what will it bring?
> At least we may be
> sure of Spring!
> What will they hold,
> the coming hours?
> At least we may be
> sure of flowers!
> Blossoms and birds,
> and budding trees,

Thank God we may
be sure of *these*!

And I wrote, during that last visit to see my mother:

Alone and very tired
It's a good place to Be;
and to come Home—
that part of me that seeks, Caliban-like
to be enclosed, cleft within the Tree of Life.
Not out on the branches, nesting—
the brown mother-bird, fearful for her babies,
demanding to be fed...

No, I am the little furry creature, me,
that burrows alone, making a space for living,
a hollow Tree House,
an Anchorhold,
a Refuge—but not from Myself—
rather a place to Be Myself.

After the spending and giving,
the tears, the embrace, the multitude of feeling,
Here, a place not to feel, not to think, just
to Be—
perhaps to play.
Alone and very tired,
my body responds and renews Herself,
and with Her, my soul.
The hurt outside the Home gradually fades,
even from memory for—

I am Eve, wrapped in my Mother God's hand-sewn apron.
I am a Druid priestess from the Isle of Britain, living in
cave of stone.
I am Mrs. Noah, after the flood—

I am Mary before the Angel invaded her Virgin Self
I am my own mother, after my birth, lying in, looking out
I am a little girl who sits for her picture
inviolate, innocent, full of wisdom
I am the old woman I may one day be
inviolate, innocent, full of wisdom

Yes, we can come Home again,
and sitting quietly in this Paradise place,
find Peace and Joy and Restoration.
Home is where the heart is—
and here is where I tend the Holy Hearth,
the sacred fires of my Self
Warming myself,
Nourishing myself,
Loving myself,
Being who I want to be—
Letting go of neediness,
anger and fear—even tears—
I left them outside the door
and crept into a
Safe Place.

What can the zambuk do during Holy Saturday? Jesus prayed for his disciples quite simply, without instructions to the Father or any kind of agenda: "Father, I pray for those you sent me."

"For there is hope of a tree, if it be cut down, that it will sprout again, and that the tender branch thereof will not cease" (Job 14: 7).

Prayer is needed now.

The time of the dove is not an easy peace. The common saying "You might as well kill two birds with one stone" reminds us that pigeon pie was a staple diet for ordinary people, especially in Northern Europe: killing birds has been a common practice. The little, sprouting, delicate crocus can easily be crushed underfoot. Many fragments are coming together at this time for the celebrant: reconciliation of "the two silences."

Francis Kline, O.C.S.O., abbot of Mepkin Abbey in South Carolina, describes this process:

> The human condition is the most inexplicable when needless and unmerited suffering gets heaped up on people when they are the most vulnerable. As an adult, the most difficult thing I have to do is to try and get in touch with my childhood pain. When I saw a child receive abuse when he looked for love, get a snake when she asked for bread, I used to feel outrage. Then I realized that outrage is my own cumulative reaction to any and all cruelty I myself have suffered. The violence which people commit and for which they are imprisoned is the pent-up rage of violence done to them when they were defenseless. Even my own cruelty I now see to be not so much an immediate reaction to cruelty done to me right now, but the pushing of the button on old pain, a reenactment of a scene which happened long ago which, when activated in the present, spins me into action like a wind-up toy. So now, when I see cruelty, or read of it, or suffer it myself, instead of riding high on my justifiable rage, I have seen that the bravest thing to do is to notice the suffering of the child, and take it into myself. I want to notice how the child immediately interiorizes the pain—does not fight back or retort in any way. The child cannot fight back an adult, one who holds the key of life and death over him. The child is silent and isolated as the pain goes in deep like a splinter, there to fester, poisoning the precious fibers of goodness and trust with which the child was born.

We all are drawn to the soft-spoken voice of one who has suffered, either in a concentration camp, or on a hospital bed, or after a traumatic experience. For the voice seems to come to us from beyond this world, from that place where body and soul are torn apart. We must and do have great respect for one who has been through such an experience. The speech of such a one is redolent with it.

Out of this silence comes a willingness to accept the *blessing* of the wound. I have realized that the healing power that was born of my abuse is the wisdom of my own Aphrodite-actress-style sexuality. Aphrodite (or Venus in Roman times) was the alchemic goddess, and I begin to recognize and use these gifts. Now I *choose* to use them, relying on my intuitive feelings.

Last Good Friday, I found myself in the Cathedral of St. John the Divine, in New York City, around 9:00 a.m. As you know, not much happens in our churches before noon on that day, but the homeless were already at prayer. I fell into deep conversation with a young mother out begging for food for her children; I gave her all the money that I had on me (it wasn't much!). Around the corner in the cathedral, propped up against one of the giant pillars, was another homeless person, an older man, black—with the most extraordinarily alive eyes and the warmest smile. He asked me for money; I said I had none. But then I felt a real attraction to him. (Yes, it was sexual!) So I knelt in front of him and said, "But I can give you a kiss!"—and I did! It was powerful and passionate—and *not* from pity. I recognized in him a kindred spirit. "I love you, lady," he said. As I walked away from him, I turned and called out, "I love you too!" A passing sacristan nearly fainted! The remembrance of that, my Good Friday "Love Affair," brings me deep abiding peace. The roots of that heightened sexual awareness go back to my childhood. I am at home in my body in the same way my father was in his youth and in his mellow old age.

My dear friend Phyllis speaks of her early maturity that grew out of her dealings with an abusive mother. She remembers her sister Nancy, age two in her high chair, eating *only* beets. She was on a "food jag"—a common occurrence around this age. Her frustrated and abusive mother had tried force-feeding her with other foods to no avail—and now set about to beat the child over the head. Phyllis, the older sister at age ten, came up behind her mother and held her wrists until the violence was restrained. Time and time again, she had to intervene in this way. In the School of Hard Knocks, she learned to handle difficult people. And now in midlife, Phyllis can sail into a room full of hostile people and take charge of the meeting in ways that astonish the more gently reared. Said Abraham Heschel:

> Between the dawn of childhood and the door
> of death, man encounters things and events out
> of which comes a whisper of truth, not much
> louder than stillness, but exhorting and persis-
> tent. Yet man listens to his fears and his whims,
> rather than to the gentle petitions of God. The
> Lord of the universe is suing for the favor of
> man.

Phyllis has come to the place of the dove through the painful process of "holding fast"—and through deepening prayer and slow realization of her gifts: the blessed wound.

Perhaps the most difficult part of this journey for me has been dealing with what I call my "Inquisition." Like Teresa of Avila, who was constantly grilled throughout her adventurous and stormy life by the people in the church who saw her as suspect, I have been constantly questioned about my insistence that forgiveness is central to healing. Surprisingly enough, many "inquisitors" sit in high places in the church, or they are leaders in the realm of psychology. They relegate forgiveness, especially for the perpetrator, to the sidelines of life. I understand that many victims of child abuse have been pressured to forgive *before they are ready*—but let me state, as clearly as I can, how I feel about this:

• I am telling you of my experience with *my* dad. This is my story and bears no reflection on *your* experience unless you *choose* to see it that way. I am merely telling you my truth as I see it...

• ...which is, that my dad, like most perpetrators, was "victim" himself. If you have any doubt about the both/and nature of the abuse, go and visit a local jail and talk to child molesters. You may be surprised. They are nice guys—*and* child molesters. Forgiveness makes accountability absolutely *essential*—everything out in the open.

• Forgiveness flows in both directions as a gift of the Holy Spirit, and while it is true that it is often impaired by anger and denial, blame and shame, it is not a one-time thing. It runs like silver thread throughout the entire Bible—and like quicksilver in the life of Jesus of Nazareth. I believe I began to forgive my father the Sunday after the first time the abuse occurred, when we all went fishing—and it continues beyond the grave. I feel it now. And I hope he will forgive me, for any misinterpretations or "embroidered" little truths in this book.

• The moments of grace and forgiveness from childhood are *more* potent than the harm of the abuse—if we allow the Holy Spirit to bring them to full flower. "In these truths, stay and grow," says Julian. It is the power of *ruth*—a lovely medieval word. In twentieth-century English, we have kept its negative counterpart: "*ruth*less." We know a spiritual freedom...

• ...which allows us to stand firm and to make boundaries, choose our battles, our good silence and solitude, even when ruthless ones impose their cacophony and what Francis Kline calls "The Great Trial." Jesus's silence and solitude in the midst of his time of trial was born of patience and understanding.

• This is the peace that Jesus breathes into his disciples after his Resurrection, when the disciples are locked in fear with the doors barred (John 20:19-23). He says, "Receive the Holy Spirit. If you forgive the sins of any, they are forgiven; if you retain the sins of any, they are retained." Having experienced this liberation, we can never go backwards. We have come full circle: we have regained our true virginity, we are "as little children." Remember that Jesus chose to show his wounds to only *a selected few*. He did not appear to multitudes in public places like the temple. Fame would have ruined it all.

• Mary Magdalene, like Janet, "held fast" through her time of trial with her seven demons, and then, in the garden after the Resurrection, Jesus tells her "Don't hold me, for I have not yet ascended to my Father and your Father." The freedom that forgiveness bestows allows us to go in peace to another dimension beyond.

I have experienced this in acting. In the play I perform as Julian of Norwich, the playwright, J. Janda, imagines that the mother of the priest, John Ball (a medieval Archbishop Romero, brutally murdered during the Peasant's Revolt), is brought to Julian's anchorhold for "ghostly counsel." Julian merely takes the deranged and desperate woman, puts her to bed, bids her listen to the rain outside the window, and promises her hot chicken broth and fresh baked bread in the morning. "...[F]or in that wretched woman was a God-will that never assented to sin—Just as every mother is more mindful of her dying child, than of its survivors, so too, God our Mother would embrace and cling to that good woman, and with a Mother Love keep her full surely." God, the Creator, the Lover, the Sustainer will bring John Ball's mother to her Resurrection...and all of us.

Perhaps you, as zambuk, have already realized the paradigm shift in your relationship with the celebrant. What happens to me during the scene of John Ball's mother in performing "Julian" is that I have become the "child" and the audience must now "mother" me. As I begin the play, particularly in a church setup where the audience is visible to the actress, I must act as "father" of the family gathered here, commanding their attention, hushing the world outside the play, drawing them into the experience of Julian's life. The audience, playing the other characters in the show as they listen, are my "children," victims if you will, to the storyteller's spell. After two powerful stories—one, of Julian's memories of the three outbreaks of the plague that she experienced, at age six, age nineteen, and just before her vision in her late twenties (she is a survivor too); the other, a reenactment of some of the most dramatic scenes of her vision—Julian again addresses the audience, but this time "as mother." Her "children" need a recess, and so she feeds them with milk and honey in little cups (I have audience members perform this ritual). This is the closest thing we have to the taste of mother's milk; we can survive on this.

Now the audience settles in for the second part of the play, and I can almost reach out and touch the changed atmosphere. The disturbance that the milk-and-honey break has created is quieted by a simple, time-honored method—humor. Shakespeare brings in the drunken comic Porter after Macbeth kills Duncan, and I, in pantomime, go through the impatient, frustrating ritual of "threading a needle." In the end, I give up, look out into the audience, choose a "sister"—or "brother"—and bring the imaginary cotton and needle to them for better threading. I always choose just the right person! I have never been refused, in all my hundreds of performances. The laughter and warmth this moment creates establishes a new sibling relationship between Julian and her "even-Christian sisters and brothers." In fact, we are now cocelebrants, in a post-Resurrection story. This prepares the audience to receive John Ball's mother and grow in strength to parent her pain. By the end of the play, I am the Little Child/Wise Woman Julian, who needs the care and love and even the applause of the audience. They rise to the occasion.

I believe this process also takes place in other forms of solo performance. I have seen concert pianists, conductors, singers, artists, sculptors, writers all appear before the audience at the end of a "Showing" as "little children"—the audience as solicitous as a grandmother or grandfather. "I think you need a hug and a nice cup of tea!" says the kind lady who sat in the front pew. "Here, let me take care of that suitcase of yours!" says the big, burly man who sat in the back, by the door.

To allow ourselves to be cared for, cherished, enfolded in love is the message of all the Resurrection stories of the Gospel. It is the message of the time of the dove. Luke's account of the Resurrection includes a story in which Jesus asked his incredulous disciples, "Have you anything to eat?" They offered him a piece of fish they had cooked, which he took and ate before their eyes. And he said to them, "This is what I meant by saying..." (Luke 24:41-44). Can you see him enjoying fish (maybe a Galilean eel?), wiping his fingers as he tries to explain? This is all very ordinary, homey stuff—and when we have experienced these "simple gifts," then we begin to experience freedom from the past.

> 'Tis a gift to be simple,
> 'Tis a gift to be free,
> 'Tis a gift to come down
> Where we ought to be.
> And when we find ourselves
> In the place just right
> 'Twill be in the Valley of
> Love and Delight.
> When true simplicity is gained
> To bow and to bend we shall not be ashamed,
> To turn, turn is all our Delight,
> For in turning, turning,
> We come down right.
>
> —traditional Shaker hymn

This is Janet's gift, for holding fast ("turning"), she is coming down "right." Doves mate for life, cooing with one another in the dovecote like the lover and the beloved in the "Songs of Songs." They make untidy, haphazard nests, perhaps knowing that we are all sojourners in this land. True simplicity, says the Shaker hymn, is "gained." It is a costly peace, and one that cannot be clutched at. "Holding fast" means we must still stand our ground—but with outstretched arms to let the dove fly free. The mourning dove, the carrier pigeon—they fly straight as an arrow, a symbol for peace since the days of Noah and the flood, when the dove brought news of coming home to dry land. This is the disturbing peace that the Resurrection brings. Matthew 28:8 says, "They hurried away from the tomb in awe and great joy, and ran to tell the disciples. Suddenly, Jesus was there in their path."

There is a sense of immediacy in the life of the celebrant now. They have wings; they can fly. Suddenly Christ surprises us! Yet this newfound serenity is gained only by an acceptance of the newly found self—a forgiveness that permeates the untidy nest, and the world beyond.

Henri Nouwen describes this dove nest as "hospitality of the heart." As host/hostess bird, we create a climate in which *all* are welcome to the nest. I have to credit Stephanie Crumley-Effinger, a Quaker at Earlham College, who acted as zambuk to me when I was behaving like a cuckoo! Cuckoos like to oust any other species of bird from the nest! The dove creates a nest that will include those just beginning the "journey" ("I only remembered two weeks ago"—eyes brimming with fear), those full of anger ("I think all perpetrators should be strung up and left to die a long, slow death!"), and those on the brink of the river of eels ("I just heard that my dad is dying. I haven't seen him in fifteen years, but somehow I feel as if I want to…").

Can all these hurting, healing birds come within the shadow of the wings of the mother-bird, brooding over the nest, until they are ready to fly? Will the other parent-bird (the zambuk) help the host/hostess bird? She needs time out for her own peace of mind and body. When the fledglings are hatched, such souls are hungry for hope, but they cannot choke themselves on unpalatable spiritual food. They will either push it away like one-year-olds or vomit like bulimic adolescents—usually all over your nice celebrant robes!

For those who find the Enneagram a helpful tool, your nest will look a lot like your redeemed number—where you go in a *good* space. My bad space (number two) means that I create chaos and trouble by my "Can I help you, poor soul?" stance. The elf song from my childhood—"This is what we do as elves,/Think of others, not ourselves"—dances through my head. In contrast, I fly straight to my (number one) True Self when I follow my gut reaction—my good angel voices of making perfect the ordinary, everyday life experience.

I just received a letter from a group of valiant souls at St. Martins-in-the-Field Church outside Philadelphia, asking me for my "Framework for Healing" to use in their beautiful healing services for survivors of cruelty and child abuse. They like my nest and want the pattern! What a compliment!

To let go of the confusion, the self-condemnation, the blame, the shame requires a conscious effort on the part of all disciples. When the shame is experienced as a belief that the core of the inner being is bad, only Love (stronger than death) can turn this around. Is this what Jesus is doing with Peter on the beach in that wonderful, funny, everyday miracle with the 153 fishes (they counted them!) described in John 21:1-19? The task besetting Peter and the others is to figure out how to get through another day, minute by minute. They need a reason to live another day. Jesus gives them one—and promises Peter and us that we *are* worthwhile. Peter the fisherman is hardly experienced as a good *shepherd.* He who is accustomed to water and nets and slippery fish must now ground himself in order "to feed sheep and lambs." Yet Jesus, the Good Shepherd, has just prepared a cooked fish, like a good fishwife, and fed Peter! He has given Peter familiar food, before asking him to extend himself beyond the "nest." What a paradox this is!

It is a threatening thing to integrate ourselves into a peaceful whole so "the fisherman part" of ourselves can become "the shepherd." Some very wounded souls, like those with multiple personality disorder, may never become "*one* story." (They are like a collection of short stories.) Yet Jesus seems to suggest that there can be a *healthy* splitting, when we make a conscious choice to do so. Here he is giving Peter the chance to choose love that is so real, so centered in the Christ, that it will extend beyond our little nest—like lives—and fly onwards and upwards.

The Holy Spirit is not languishing in a miserable cage at the mercies of the dove sellers, who would kill her/him as a sacrifice. This is not the sacrifice that God requires of us; it is the spiritual freedom to, day by day, *choose* life.

Peter does not do this alone. His support system—the other disciples, wife, mother-in-law, and family members—is now in place. He has 153 fishes as well! Community is what is to come at Pentecost—when the gathered disciples, the company of women, Mary in their midst, climbed the stairs to that upper room, to await the promised Holy Spirit. Con-celebrants all, they sat in that peaceful place, in prayer and patient expectation and hope. Among them was Thomas (and there will always be a "Thomas"!). The story of doubting Thomas (John 20:26-29) is repeated over and over again. Thomas needs proof. He is an eighteenth century man in many ways—very rational, very reasonable. Jesus, the patient teacher, comes to show Thomas his Blessed Wounds—and Thomas immediately becomes a mystic: "My Lord and my God!" We do not even hear that he needs to accept Jesus's invitation: "Put your finger here and see my hands; and put out your hand and place it in my side; do not be faithless, but believing...."

At a retreat I once led for survivors, one woman became predictably incensed when I mentioned forgiveness. (I've learned there are several such in every group.) I refused to back down from my position, insisting that forgiveness of *self* was essential—and then forgiveness for others may well be given. She was adamant! She would *never* forgive (not even herself)! Over a year later, this same woman drove for two hours to my show on Mary, the mother of Jesus (*Blessed!*), to tell me of a miracle of faith: she had found forgiveness for herself *and* her father! And Mary, who perhaps knows more about forgiveness than anyone else who ever lived, smiled on both of us, remembering perhaps her own difficult "peace," forged in anguish after she watched her son laid in a borrowed tomb and learned second-hand about the Resurrection. There is a reason the canon of the Gospels are *silent* on Mary's part in the post-Resurrection stories, for she has the task of mothering the church into being—which includes *all* of us. (In my imagination, Mary is consoling the family of Judas Iscariot on Easter morning and that is why she is not in the garden with the other women.)

Does this Easter morning peace extend to the perpetrator as well?

How can we help the abuser to heal—as a faithful community diligently seeking out the lost sheep—and not relegate this serious charge to the secular and legalistic world? Is it enough for the church to sit back and sigh in relief after the trial is over and the perpetrator has been thrown into jail—perhaps leaving spouse, children, and a trail of dependent, unhappy victims in the wake?

I believe the church in the past, when she had perhaps greater powers, was better equipped to deal with "notorious sinners," as our 1928 Prayer Book puts it, than we are today. We are so heavily into denial that we are happy to think that child molesters can now go to jail, and all we have to do is just send the chaplain in to visit occasionally.

The need for forgiveness of the perpetrators is often so desperate that a great Lenten-type discipline is required—one that tests the imagination and loving concern of the whole church. In a sense, they need to be "defrocked"—stripped naked—to understand their shame in a healthy way and then come to repentance. If child molesters had been in the crowd that approached John the Baptist at the Jordan River, asking him, "What should we do?" I believe he might have replied that they must accept some act of public humiliation. I believe, in his heart of hearts, my father would have welcomed it. I read that a judge in a recent court case involving a "notorious sinner" offered him the choice of castration or life imprisonment; he chose castration! How barbaric! What a sad reflection on the life of the church, that that is the best we can do! I think Christ Jesus offers us a better way by far. But as a community, we need to bring the peace of Christ to all.

I can imagine that if you are a pastor of a large church, you might ask yourself how you could possibly initiate this? Should we wait for church leaders to create the atmosphere in which such "sinners" are brought to the altar call? Of course, it must begin with the *public* admission that *all* have sinned and fallen short of God's glory. So the good shepherd who would search diligently for the lost sheep must first rend his or her own heart—and openly confess before brothers and sisters that we are *all* abusive, *all* perpetrators, of one kind or another. We have met the enemy, and he or she is us. It is as if the devil stands above us, flogging us from on high with all the shame-filled lies of the past. To let go of that whip may mean years of repeating over and over again "You are beautiful—you are worthwhile—you are loved—you are lovable!" so that gradually the voices to the contrary grow softer and softer.

Last Ash Wednesday, I led a Lenten retreat day at a seminary. (I believe that seminarians—and people in ministry, in general—may have suffered a higher percentage of child abuse than any other group in the country.) We spent the afternoon in solitude, writing down all the lies we had ever heard about ourselves and about God—and then we brought them to a brazier set up in the middle of the chapel. We stood in a circle and, one by one, burnt these lies. I invited whoever wished to read the lies aloud before burning them—and over and again, we heard the familiar voices of condemnation: You are stupid! You are no good! God won't like you. You are dirty…a bastard…a fool…ignorant! God is mad at you. You are not worthy…"

The gift of my little sister, Jessica, to my dad was that he was able to shower her with all the tender mercy he held within his own heart. Here was someone who was palpably weaker, dependent entirely on his care and attention. He did not molest Jessica. Being so severely spastic, she did not "see" in our sense of the word. (I always used to say she looked at me as if I were a table; there was no recognition of a *person* in her eyes.) Yet my dad, in his creative, playful way, was absolutely wonderful with Jessica. He could make her laugh, because he treated her like a darling little creature, pouring out all the affection onto her that he so desperately needed for himself. He would start at her toes and kiss her gently all the way up her body to the top of her head! How do I know that kissing did not include her private parts? I just do. I know him. I swear to it.

Maybe the offer of celibacy in a monastic community could provide a framework in which child molesters would "repay" the debt to society. I can see the prisoners that I know at Avenel—the Adult Diagnostic and Treatment Center—being gainfully employed as monks, helping to care for handicapped people in a carefully supervised and prayerful community. The possibilities are endless. I am sure they are not original—and perhaps in the past some of the greatest Christian minds were put to work because of an abusive past, a past that was gently laid to rest within the embrace of a religious community. St. Augustine? It is interesting that our "Anglican Augustine"—John Donne—came to the fullness of his spirituality *after* the death of his wife, Ann, when he became celibate and understood that "No man is an island, entire of himself...Ask not for whom the bell tolls. It tolls for thee."

The one who tastes the greatest pain and shame often knows the deepest joy. In reading the *Confessions* of St. Augustine or the poems and sermons of John Donne, one senses a turbulent spirit that has plummeted to the depths of self-hatred and despair in matters of sexuality and is now coming up into the rarefied air of the Holy Spirit. Both of these great souls found their home within the church. It is said of John Donne that he walked up and down the nave of St. Paul's Cathedral, London, every afternoon for a space of three hours making himself available for spiritual counseling to anyone who wished to accost him. He became a zambuk! Would twentieth century bishops and deacons of cathedrals lay themselves open to such daily "good Samaritan-ing?"

At the end of her life, St. Teresa of Avila wrote, "Finally, Lord, I am a daughter of the church." These are the words of a woman at peace with herself. Within my own journey—which has included forgiving the church for her treatment of victims of child abuse, in particular, and women, in general—I believe I too have come to lay aside some of my own anger, my denial, my oppression. I cannot do otherwise—I am a daughter of the church too! To let go of the shame and blame for my own Anglican corner of Christendom is a great relief! I even lay aside a part of my feminism. I will die for Jesus—but not for feminism! It is the un-Christ-like parts of any cause or concern that must be surrendered—even my enormous, long list of "What I Would Want the Church To Do About Child Sexual Abuse." I simply submit that agenda to Jesus, who smiles kindly at me—and then gives me a wink!

It is this hope and joy, the fruit of holding fast—through Lent to Easter "showings"—that can take us to the last days of the journey: The Mystical Swan.

hold me fast
don't let me
pass

IX THE SWAN:

TRUST—
IN GOD,
IN SELF,
IN OTHERS

On the day of Dad's funeral in England, I performed *Masks and Mirrors* at a little Congregational church in Salisbury, Connecticut. About a hundred people gathered. It was a sacred experience. After it was over, there was a silence, and then I invited questions from the audience. The first one, from a man sitting in the front row, was "Is your father still alive?" What made it possible for me to tell my story so that I felt strengthened and empowered and that man and others felt consoled and renewed?

I believe what made it possible was the fact that I am now not merely "survivor" but "celebrant." Let me tell you how I came to this priestly role.

In her book on the prayer life of the people of the Hebrides (those remote islands to the northwest of Scotland), Esther de Waal describes a process used in weaving called "waulking": "...stretching the cloth on a frame to strengthen and thicken it, a communal activity that gave rise to waulking songs, sung by a group of women. One of them, the consecrator—or celebrant— would lead a ceremony at sunrise, placing the roll of cloth in the center of the frame, turning it slowly, and naming each member of the household for whom it was intended, then reversing it, in the name of the Father, Son, and Holy Spirit. Not only is the warp and woof of every thread then consecrated to God, but also the final process takes place in God's presence and God is even assumed to be part of that process, placing an arm around each woman as she waulks."

How was the consecrator—the celebrant—"ordained," chosen from out of the midst to lead the waulking process? This song of completion and thanksgiving—how do we sing it? How can we say, like Mary, "Here I am"?

One Advent, I performed *Blessed!*, my liturgical drama on Mary, the mother of Jesus, about fifteen times. After the last performance, while I was still wearing my Queen of Heaven robes, an elderly nun came up to me and said, "So you were the celebrant!" It was a moment of insight and recognition for me, and now I feel ordained to move behind the altar of my life and offer up the sacrifices on behalf of all of us. I am "waulking"! The cloth of my life has been strengthened and thickened by all my fellow weaver-survivors. How extraordinary and rich and blessed is the fabric around this painful issue! Like David, I can also dance in front of the altar, offering thanksgiving.

Tam Lin, like Jesus, explains the nature of the holding process (the kingdom of heaven) very clearly to Janet before it all happens. There are precise instructions as to which horse, which rider, and even which signs will provide ways to recognize him "among so many strange knights I've never seen before." The right hand, gloved; the left hand, bare; the peak of the cap turned up. Likewise, "I'll comb down my hair." Janet is probably as bone weary and exhausted as I am as I get this book to Abbey

Press by the time the dove flies away into the sky. This is surely, by now, the dawn of All Saints' Day (for "at midnight, on Halloween, the fairy folk took horse"). November 1: Can you see the late fall, my favorite time of year (my birthday is November 13), chilly dawn, as a lovely swan, wings outstretched, long neck gracefully stretched towards Janet, the mate perhaps flying behind? (Swans do mate

The author's father and daughter Missy, a few months before his death.

for life, so where you find one swan, you usually find another.) Janet must stand her ground, her gaze clear into the future, for this is the last step before the final transformation. She cannot give up now. "Life must be lived forward, but it is understood backward" (Soren Kierkegaard). This is the ultimate trust in ourselves and in God. It takes great courage.

By All Saints' Day, we know that we are surrounded by a community of loving, caring souls, those we can trust. My zambuks—they are like bricks in my castle, a strong tower to uphold me. If I began to name them, what a mighty ensemble! How rich I am! I think of sitting in church one day with three friends—Pat Ferry, Pat Whitton, and Janet. All three knelt in prayer, and my eyes filled with tears of joy and love at the grace, the different beauty, of each one of them. The message of the swan is one of hope and trust. This allows us to create the necessary boundaries, the fences that were torn down and damaged when the castle fell into ruin. They can now be restored.

The two swans swimming serenely, with water flowing

between them, may be husband and wife, dentist and patient, lover and beloved, soul friends (spiritual director and directee), minister and parishioner, two men making peanut butter sandwiches at the soup kitchen, two women exercising at the spa, a babysitter and a mother enjoying a cup of coffee while the child plays. Jesus came to call us friends.

The water, or the air (for you cannot hold a swan too fast or too long), is the necessary ingredient that allows you to be you and me to be me without the encumbrances of "Fairy Land." We can be real with one another. The trust means truth. We will stumble—particularly with the "no's," for the childhood patterns of the ugly little signet are firmly entrenched and "yes, Daddy" is still easier to say than "no." But we can pick ourselves up again; trusting the *process* of healing is the final cry of the lovely swan.

This process we can hand on to generations yet unborn. To our children—biological and otherwise—we can model a way of being that engenders respect and points the way to fullness of life. This allows the child to make choices and explore new territory.

For many months when Dad was dying, my youngest brother Bruce and his wife tried as best as they could to care for him. It became very difficult. I managed four trips to England in 1990, but I had so many nonnegotiable contracts to fill in late October, I just couldn't go. Missy, my oldest daughter, called me one night: "I'm worried about Granddad. I'm going to England to see him." She was there for a week, nursing him, caring for him. I am immensely proud of her. The night of Dad's funeral, I performed *Masks and Mirrors* in Connecticut. My youngest daughter, Celia, attended the funeral in England. I am immensely proud of her. It was a great "time of trial" for both of them.

Trusting the process is trusting Tam Lin. It is the message of the Epistles of John: "That which was from the beginning, which we have heard, which we have seen with our eyes, which we have looked upon and touched with our hands" (1 John 1). "Little children, let us not love in word or speech but in deed and in truth" (1 John 3:18). "And by this we know that he abides in us by the spirit which he has given us" (1 John 3:24).

The final words of the Second Symphony (*Resurrection*) of Gustav Mahler (1860-1911) were written by Mahler himself:

CONTRALTO
O believe, my heart, o believe,
nothing of you will be lost!
What you longed for is yours,
yours what you loved,
what you championed!

SOPRANO
O believe,
you were not born in vain!
Have not vainly lived
and suffered!

CHORUS AND CONTRALTO
What was created,
that must pass away!
What passed away, must rise!
Cease to tremble!
Prepare yourself to live!

SOPRANO AND CONTRALTO
O suffering! you that pierce all things,
from you I am wrested away!
O death! you that overcome all things,
now you are overcome!
With wings that I wrested for myself
in the fervent struggle of love
I shall fly away
to the light whither no eye pierced.

CHORUS
Rise again you will

> *my heart, in a trice!*
> *What you have beaten*
> *will carry you to God.*

A child's poem tells us that this life struggle is slow "growing up" and can only come with the tranquility of the swan-like spirit even in the midst of life's hurly-burly.

> There go the grown-ups to the office, to the store,
> Subways crush, traffics rush,
> Hurry, Worry, Scurry, Flurry!
> No wonder grown-ups don't grow up anymore.
> It takes a lot of SLOW to GROW.

> Slow as a swan gliding across a lake!

We begin to see ourselves, as in a mirror's true reflection. To know, like Ann Frank, that "in spite of everything, people are really good at heart" is to know oneself, to keep forgiving oneself over and over again. Accepting the confusion that still lies deep within the soul—as chaotic as a young girl torn away from home and forced into a dreadful exile in Nazi Holland or a little girl (myself) who repeated the pattern of abuse with her father over and over again with friends' uncles, boyfriends, Gethsemani Abbey monks, husband, children—and yet know that at the core of my being is the inviolate true self—this is *trust*.

So often we have taught ourselves to believe the voices of rejection, and then we hate ourselves for what is only learned behavior. No wonder others draw back in horror when we are often so hard, so judgmental of ourselves. This is a *very, very, very* slow process, which means we nibble at the nourishing Bread of Life a little at a time, rather as a swan or a duck feeds. The "feast or famine" dramas of the mighty lion are laid to rest. For the power struggles are now replaced with "the little light of our understanding." I do not believe that dominance and control (power issues) can be answered by grabbing, clutching, wresting the power away from "the enemy." To love our enemies, we must replace any longing for vengeance with understanding. How can we know and understand others if we have so little self-knowledge? And this takes time.

In order to keep this book truthful to the end, I spent four hours at Avenel, interviewing five of the prisoners there and talking with some of the staff. I will be returning next month to do my show again, for this is my best audience. (Perhaps I'll work in drama with them as the actors later this year.)

Let me give you a few excerpts from the wisdom of Avenel. (The names have been changed.)

The author, at age six-and-a-half, and her brother Bill, at one-and-a-half, before the abuse.

Robert (mid-thirties, dark hair, bearded, handsome, articulate): He had a workaholic, absent father and an abusive mother. His only friend as a child was a little girl, Jeanine, who moved away when he was six. They would huddle together, crying, clutching each other, at an old brewery, their play yard. He was sexually abused by his kindergarten teacher. The only good sexual experience was with Jeanine, the child. He became fixated on the idea that in order to get the cuddling and stroking he so desperately needed, it could only come through children. He could not trust women (they reject him or beat him or abuse him). He could not trust men (they are absent). But he could make children love him, because he could give them sex and make them both feel good. "I was bad. I was unlovable, and only a child could

227

love me, so this intensified sex-play. Children won't reject me. Not having love is like dying for a child. As my courage increases, I know God will not allow me to go through something I can't handle. Trust and forgiveness. That's it!"

Kevin (late sixties, dignified, a studious, learned man, transparent spirituality; I'd cast him for Prospero if ever I do *The Tempest* at Avenel): He was deeply touched by the pure innocence of the baby mask underneath the perpetrator in my show. His advice for people on the outside: "Hear my side of the story too. Walk a mile in my moccasins. I did not become a sex-offender overnight. I was trained to do it. I resisted acting-out for forty years, and then the volcano erupted. Do you have a volcano inside you? Find a safe place for it. I have become more trusting of myself, and the key, of course, is forgiveness."

Evan (mid-sixties, been in and out of prison for most of his adult life, in and out of institutions as a child; only thing he held onto was work; did not learn to read or write until thirty, when he was in Trenton State Prison; tried hard to be a good parent; had several children): He said, "No more Dr. Jekyll and Mr. Hyde! I'm tired of all the violence. A.A. is my backbone. I know I'm a good worker. That gives me self-respect. The first time I came here, I was three years in denial. I accept what I cannot change. One day at a time, that gives me peace. The biggest part is forgiveness."

You could hear the refrain, over and over again, in each man's story: I am learning to forgive myself for the sins I commit that are part of the fabric of my childhood. I know I must not torture myself through stifling the reflection that I begin to see—in the lake of my life and in you, my sister.

What I sensed in these men was balance—an integration of darkness and light. I think many of us could empathize with this English Quaker:

COLOURING
Perhaps the most prominent colouring of
taught Christianity for me has been its emphasis

upon purity and perfection, often represented as "light," and its fear of and hostility towards darkness. Darkness, however, is as important as light for survival and growth of living things, which need both. Injunctions to turn away from darkness and towards the light, or calls in a more militant vein for the light to overcome the darkness, deny this truth. They also neglect a crucial quality of light: that it enables us to see what is in the darkness—though not of course, if we have turned from it and are looking the other way.

Coming out of Avenel to "the world outside," I was immediately assaulted by the realization that we live in a world that cannot cope with the darkness and which projects so many negative feelings on "the abuser," because the mirror is so smudgy for ourselves.

We may want to "hate" our perpetrators, never to trust them again, but then how can we ever love God, whom we have not seen, if we cannot love our neighbor, especially if he or she is languishing in jail? Can we on the outside ever trust the abuser again? Many child molesters do keep repeating, like my dad. It was not only Missy and me—also cousins, a school friend, and other girls. You could say that my trust in my dad was misplaced. I don't think it was, because the trust was *not* in the abuse but in the essential goodness (the "God-will" within my dad) that finally triumphed over the other side of him.

One night when I was visiting my dad in England, in the summer of 1990, he was in such terrible pain with the cancer (before the morphine) that, brave as he was, he said he was going "to throw in his fishing rods" himself if this kept up. I was sleeping in my parents' bedroom and Dad was on a sofa bed in the living room of his mobile home. As anyone knows who has "watched through the night" with a pain-filled person, "sleeping" is a euphemism. I was beside myself wondering how I could divert the pain. Suddenly, standing by his bedside, I knew what I had to do. "Move over, Dad," I said, "I'm coming in bed with you." All that night, I held him close to me and kissed and soothed the pain and told him funny stories. We planned his funeral and sang hymns, trying to choose the right ones: "I know, how about 'Abide with Me'?" "No, that won't do." "'Rock of Ages'?" "How about 'Fairest Lord Jesus'?" In the silences between the laughter, Dad asked me in his understated British way, "Do you mind? Is it all right for you? Now?" "Yes, Dad, it's fine now." And it was. At dawn, he finally fell into a deep sleep.

When the priest, Father Roger—a jolly fellow rather like the clergyman, Reverend Mr. Beeb, in the film *A Room With a View*—arrived with communion, he did not raise an eyebrow seeing father and daughter in bed together. I had confided in him, and he told me that he would make available the confessional to Dad. I happen to know that Dad took advantage of the offer, and Father Roger was just the right kind of zambuk for him. When I told him of the incest, he said, "Oh, yes, lots of that around. I taught in a boys' school for years. I was always hearing about it. Confession is the best thing when he's ready."

Dad was ready. Such intimacy is what Julian is speaking about when she says, "We can be so close to God that there is nothing in between us." With this kind of trust, deep and abiding, we can move mountains. In the Acts of the Apostles, those shame-filled men like Peter and James are transformed into eloquent miracle workers. What amazing grace that can immediately free paralyzed limbs and send them leaping and laughing through the temple, as in Acts 3:1-10.

Jesus had promised those who witnessed his outrage in the temple before the crucifixion that he would restore the temple of God in three days. Here was living proof! This "temple" (our bodies too) can be freed up by strong, loving, helpful hands if only we choose to live, to forgive. One of the sad things that I often encounter is that survivors have made that choice, but it has been smothered, extinguished, by impatience and despair or just plain old negative thinking (often by well-meaning zambuks) so they cannot be celebrants.

At a recent one-day healing conference at the Cathedral of Christ the King at Kalamazoo, Michigan, where over three-hundred people from all denominations (and none) gathered, Abbot Andrew, from the Benedictine (Episcopalian) Abbey at Three Rivers, and I were speaking with a young mother, a single parent with two little children, who was severely wounded herself. She had suffered ritual abuse. (This is the most appalling of abuse. One can only stand in awe and humility before such extraordinary suffering at the hands of the devil.) The woman knew she was recycling the pain in spite of all kinds of secular therapy. She desperately needed to move on.

A recent photo of the author's daughter Celia, at age 21.

I sensed Father Andrew's deep, kindly listening—a gift that only he could share with her. So I left the two of them—the woman crying, stuck in her pain—and went upstairs to the sanctuary to pack up my things. It was a hasty piece of praying that I did right then. Distance was very important. About thirty minutes later, I came downstairs and found a miracle! The woman had stopped crying and there was a light in her eyes. Father Andrew looked drained but peaceful. He wrote to me:

"So far, my pastoral experience has been that recovery tends to be very slow and it cannot be rushed. It seems that one must be obedient to the pain and to that pain's own pace for healing. Victims and healers alike would like the process to be faster than it usually is. I feel the Lord is teaching us some of the more profound reaches of patience."

I had the sense that a link in the chain of abuse had been weakened. Please pray for her and her little son, Zachary (age

The author and her husband on their wedding day.

six). Will they take up the abbot's invitation and spend a few quiet days of respite at the Abbey? Perhaps. Trust in a quiet, black-robed Scotsman who will not abuse her or her children as other similarly clad but evil ones had done (black robes are part of Satanic rites) may provide a helping hand out of the pit of hell. When Julian is in the throes of death, she has a nightmare that the devil is choking her, paralyzed as she is by fear. The three people at her bedside—her mother, her priest, and a child—all say, "No! No! No!" (denying the devil). Julian has to do everything in "threes," she is so trinitarian. Suddenly she realizes that "sin" in God's eyes is nothing! *Nothing*! And the nightmare vanishes. She can fix her gaze once more upon Christ crucified but "right merry."

There is enormous joy and enthusiasm even in the midst of the martyrdom tales of Acts and the early church. There is a beautiful myth surrounding St. Polycarp, the earliest Christian martyr after St. Stephen. This reverent old man went peacefully to his funeral pyre, and as his body was consumed by flames, a white dove flew out of his heart and straight up to heaven. In such peace, the dove is transformed into the larger, lovelier black or white swan. These mystical, mythical birds do come in both colors. They are not grey, and the spirituality they suggest is like night and day. Holding fast to a swan when his or her home is the broad lake or the wide blue sky is impossible. Swans must fly and swim.

As we marvel at these elegant creatures from a distance, they can teach us much about living day to day in God's grace and favor, open to the Holy Spirit. Ducks and even swans will come to human beings and accept the bread they have to offer. Little children, in particular, enjoy feeding swans and ducks, not too close, but rewarded by lessons in contemplation and wonder that go far beyond anything we could teach them in a classroom. A swan can teach us how to pray if we watch attentively, how to choose a day-to-day, ordinary life lived in communion with the Creator, accepting both darkness and light with serenity.

Swans tell us to trust our Tam Lin wherever he or she may be found. They mate for life, and a common picture is of male and female swans swimming together as a pair. My husband of twenty-five years, Maury, is the one who has taught me about faithfulness and trust more than anyone else. Some years ago, a friend of the family (and Maury's in particular), Cliff Ettinger died very peacefully after an illness that echoed my dad's. He died well, just as he had lived well. My husband grieved for Cliff, and when we heard of his death, I wrote a short note to Cliff's brother with my remembrances of this kind, urbane, swan-like gentleman. At his funeral in a New England Congregational church, the minister read out my letter in his eulogy, and my husband broke down and sobbed in my arms. This is the most private, reserved person you could ever wish to meet, but we touched an intimacy on that occasion that was a glimpse of heaven. Later at the funeral lunch in an old Connecticut restaurant, we watched two swans on the lake beside the inn, and I knew that trust and love could be shared in ways that transcend and transform our mundane little lives.

My swan became "the prince" that day. Recognizing the prince/princess in one another brings the reward of courtesy (the manners of the "court") and respect for one another. This makes for balance in our lives. It brings wisdom. Let me quote from the play *All That I Am*, which was written for me by another swan-like person, my good friend Sister Irene Mahoney, O.S.U. St. Augustine's mistress is contrasting his search for wisdom with her own simple understanding: "Wisdom, I believe, brings peace and harmony. It takes the pieces of our lives, the jagged, the smooth, the small, the large, the heavy, the light and fits them all together into a whole as God has made our world! Sun and moon, deserts and wooded mountains, water and dry land, the world has need of all. So it is with us, the body needs the soul, the soul the body." This inclusive view of life is grounded in a center which is Christ. Swans can stand (even sleep, the zoo tells me) on one leg, perfectly balanced in a line that every ballet dancer attempts to imitate. The discipline, the pain of years of training required for this most civilized of art forms, can bring us to the perfection of *Swan Lake*. We find, as T.S. Eliot tells us, "the still point at the beginning of the world." Julian speaks of seeing God "in a pointe."

One-ness—reconciliation with God, with neighbor, and with ourselves—is the fruit of the journey. In our end is our beginning for, in finding our true self (Tam Lin), we now have to await the birth of the first child and the work of rebuilding the Castle of Carterhaugh, which, you will remember, has fallen into ruin. Life is a dance if we choose to see it that way.

The life of a Trappist monk is not often seen as a dance. But a benefactor gave Father Edward of Holy Cross Abbey in Berryville, Virginia, a $50 (no less!) ticket to the Bolshoi Ballet at the Performing Arts Center at Wolftrap near Washington D.C. last summer. It was a treat beyond all belief for him, and he was bubbling over with his transfiguration experience when I visited the monastery with my show on Teresa of Avila (another dancer!). Father Edward wrote me:

> You will be happy to know that I have "let myself go" and now dance quite regularly—on my own! It has become my custom to go for my walk when everyone has gone to bed after Compline—between 8:00 and 9:00 p.m. I walk on the paved road between the monastery and the entrance gate. There are several trees that are "friends" of mine, and my dance centers on

them. I carry a small cassette recorder in my pocket and have the headphones under my cap. When the moon is above and the clouds are "dancing," I become aware of the "cosmic dance." Our solar system is dancing. I find all this liberating because our way of life and my own disciplined training inhibited such activity.

And in a letter received yesterday: "P.S. I gave up dancing for Lent!"

This may not be your style, but we can trust in ourselves that life in the body that was once abused can be found in the most ordinary, everyday life experiences. Look around you. What you need may be found in the yellow pages of most telephone books. It may be found in your local cinema or high school or convent or next door neighbor's home.

My youngest daughter, Celia, persuaded me to join the local health spa where she is a member. Step aerobics with thirty-five sweating, panting women of all shapes, sizes, and colors (the health spa is on the border of Teaneck and Englewood, New Jersey, so the clientele is multi-racial) can bring great zest to a dreary day. One of the instructors, a petite Russian-Armenian woman, always refers to the body as "her": "All right, ladies, move her around to the other side!" And exercising to what my cousin Jake from Brooklyn calls "jungle music" puts me in touch with the real life of youth! It is a mistake to condemn all modern popular music as "bad." Listen to the lyrics; they often speak of the mystical longing of the soul for union with God, with "the other." There is a great deal more good in rock music than bad. One of the most thrilling things I ever experienced was a U-2 concert with my daughter and her friends. And to hear Celia say to my husband, "You should see Mommy at the spa; she is so darling!" makes me feel like Mrs. America, newly crowned!

What has happened to the zambuk—the con-celebrant—seeing your ugly duckling become a swan? After Pentecost, those present must have looked around in sheer wonder, sensing in others what they too had experienced. This Pentecost experience is rooted in forgiveness. The disciples, the women, could be there only because they had begun to forgive themselves. The ultimate act of trust is one's being ready to forgive oneself. I suppose Mary, Queen of Heaven, as she sits in the midst of all of our Pentecosts, is the greatest example of a person who trusted herself. She did it with her "fiat" at the Annunciation and so could take on all those "swans" in the upper room. Her support system with "all the women" was in place and "the beloved disciple" provided her with a home to return to after they descended the stairs.

This free-flowing trust permeates all our homes. For me, it is the transformation I feel within my own being that flows outwards towards all whom I love. It is the knowledge that I will not abuse my children, that the chain is forever sundered. Because I have known "the shadow" (the reflection of the swan in the lake), I can live in the light. This light shines now on a well-ordered home (I gave up trying to be superwoman, and now my good neighbor, Erika, comes and cleans my house once a week, and it is a time of sharing and caring for both of us) and a pleasant family where hospitality, even jollity, are the norm. I do not wish to give the impression that we have it all made. Retracing my steps has been a long, long process, and I am not finished yet, even if I have wrapped my Tam Lin in my green, green cloak. Rebuilding the ruined castle is full-time work, but it is a lot easier when you have your Beloved beside you to help. My Beloved is Christ.

I would like to close with Proper Twenty, prayers for the Sunday closest to September 21, in our *Book of Common Prayer*:

"Grant us Lord, not to be anxious about earthly things but to love things heavenly, and even now while we are placed among things that are passing away to hold fast to those that shall endure through Jesus Christ our Lord who lives and reigns with you and the Holy Spirit, one God for ever and ever, Amen."

Dear friends, this may seem a very dull, even boring way to end the book, but that's it: Ordinary time, after Easter, old green chasuble-celebrant robes, day-to-day stuff, but worth it!

EPILOGUE

I t was the summer of 1964, and I was traveling in Israel, staying at the Bathsheba Y, when a telegram arrived from far-
away, cold Canada. It was from a certain John Hirsch of the
Manitoba Theatre Centre. (A great theater director, he died in
1989.) I had forgotten that I had applied for the job at the Theatre
School several months previous. Was he serious? On my return
to England, all suntanned, lean, and Israelized, I found that a
whole batch of telegrams awaited me. I was summoned to the
newly opened Hilton Hotel opposite Hyde Park early the next
morning. I struggled into a pair of hose and heeled shoes and took
the train to London.

This gentle, mild, mad Jewish bird, a child of the Holocaust,
met me in the lobby and took me to lunch. We had Lord Derby's

stew, I remember. A fur fashion show was in progress, so the interview was interrupted as luscious blondes draped in minks and sables sidled up to the table to display their wares. Somewhere in between, we talked about theater and children and Life—and Life and theater and children. At the end of the lunch, John said, "Will you come?" and I said "Yes." He was returning to Winnipeg that night, he said. He wanted me there in a week's time.

I left the Hilton feeling—what? Excited, apprehensive, but mostly brave. This was pioneer stuff. I wanted to be part of the adventure, and here was a Prince of Players in the mode of the great ones that I admired the most, like Dame Edith Evans, Sir Laurence Olivier, and Dame Flora Robson. I needed to process it. I walked for hours all over London and finally found myself outside an obscure little art gallery that advertised a show of work by children. I entered and lost myself in the wonderful world of color and imagination. As I wandered from picture to picture, I suddenly came across this crouched creature—spectacles on nose, peering shortsightedly at a little papier-mâché sculpture. It was John Hirsch. When he straightened up and met my eyes, he showed no surprise at seeing me here. It was the affirmation of one wounded child to another. Look, he seemed to say to me, we have come through, you and I and the children, in spite of all the unspeakable horror and tragedy. He smiled at me, eyes shining. Neither of us spoke.